empowering adhd organization and cleaning

STOP DROWNING IN OVERWHELM: THE 28-DAY WORKBOOK FOR A CLUTTER-FREE HOME, CLEAR MIND, AND PRODUCTIVE LIFE

ESTELLE ROSE

ROSALI PUBLISHING

praise for estelle rose

 Yasmine

★★★★★ **Very helpful**
Reviewed in the United States on May 18, 2025

I've tried so many planners, hacks, and routines that never really stuck—but this one actually gets how my brain works.

 Thrilling Reads With D

★★★★★ **Quick Wins for ADHD: A Must-Read Resource for Organizing Your Life and Mind**
Reviewed in the United States on January 21, 2025
Verified Purchase

"If you've ever struggled with organizing your life, decluttering your mind, or just navigating the ADHD rollercoaster, this book is a must-read. As someone diagnosed with ADHD and executive functioning disorder as a preteen, I've always struggled!"

 Lindsey W

★★★★★ **Concrete strategies to improve executive function!**
Reviewed in the United States on January 22, 2025
Verified Purchase

Estelle is the master of concrete suggestions for tackling ADHD.

 Rebecca Holmes

★★★★★ **Spoke to Me!**
Reviewed in the United States on January 11, 2025
Verified Purchase

"I felt like she had a view into my brain, she described ADHD day to day thoughts so well."

 Connie Newell

★★★★★ **Nothing short of a life-changing guide for anyone navigating the complexities of ADHD.**
Reviewed in the United States on January 21, 2025
Verified Purchase

"This book isn't just another self-help title; it's a comprehensive toolkit packed with actionable strategies, relatable insights, and empowering advice to transform daily struggles into meaningful progress."

 MGA86

★★★★★ **Practical, realistic, and actually kind to my ADHD brain**
Reviewed in the United States on April 27, 2025

This didn't try to "fix" me , it gave me tools that actually work with how I think. The small wins each week made a big difference without overwhelming me. Highly recommend if you're tired of feeling like a broken productivity robot.

 Hi'D's Book Hub - Blogger

★★★★★ **Embrace your uniqueness!**
Reviewed in the United States on October 22, 2024
Verified Purchase

"After reading Estelle Rose's book, I felt a genuine connection to her and others like me. She taught me how to apply certain insights from the book to my daily life. I appreciated that it wasn't just a book but also a workbook designed to enhance my understanding."

 dorianhellfire

★★★★★ **So helpful and relatable**
Reviewed in the United States on October 20, 2024
Verified Purchase

"Thank you for making this book! As someone who's discovering what it means to live with ADHD, this book has been a wonder to have."

 Aleisha Wilhite
★★★★★ **Helpful book**
Reviewed in the United States on August 28, 2024
Verified Purchase

"If I could sum up the book's essence in one word it would be EYE-opening."

 Megan Wilson
★★★★★ **Life-Changing**
Reviewed in the United States on October 23, 2024
Verified Purchase

"The author's tone made reading this book easy and fun. Since she has ADHD herself, I found it to be relatable, funny, and encouraging. I'm grateful for the work she's doing to help women like me."

 Tay
★★★★★ **Exceptional writing and author!**
Reviewed in the United States on April 14, 2024
Verified Purchase

"I really appreciate how the author was able to put so much in this book, she is personable and relatable. The book is very easy to read and understand. Where was this book when I was in grade school? Definitely one of the best self-help books I have read."

 Briony Anderson
★★★★★ **The only book for ADHD I'll read**
Reviewed in Australia on 28 July 2023
Verified Purchase

"I love how Estelle talks not only about why implementing some of these changes can be beneficial, she also provides step by step instructions and resources you can follow to actually stay motivated in keeping these healthy changes."

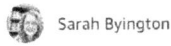 Sarah Byington

Friendly & Engaging Guide to Managing ADHD
Reviewed in the United States on August 21, 2023
Verified Purchase

"This book has been a great resource for navigating my ADHD. It is written in a friendly tone that that makes it easy to read and I didn't feel bombarded by too much information at a time. The illustrations are a helpful addition."

 G. Wagstaff

Most helpful book I've read about ADHD
Reviewed in the United Kingdom on 15 February 2024
Verified Purchase

"All I can say is that as I was reading this book, I felt like Estelle was actually talking to me. And trying to help me. I keep this book handy because I dip into it whenever I feel like I'm all over the place (which is quite often). It grounds me. Thank you, Estelle."

 Catherine S

Basically seeing someone write my life!
Reviewed in the United Kingdom on 5 January 2024
Verified Purchase

"I am not a reader - I just don't have the concentration to read. I read this book in a few hours; this never happens!"

 Tina

Great intro to ADHD
Reviewed in Canada on July 28, 2023
Verified Purchase

"This book is written in such a user friendly and engaging way. I found it very helpful as someone new to ADHD and trying to learn as much as possible as quickly as possible. This book is a great starting off point with lots of helpful examples of lived experience and ideas on how to adapt to challenges."

Copyright © 2025 by Estelle Rose - All rights reserved.

No part of this publication may be reproduced, stored or transmitted in any form or by any means, electronic, mechanical, photocopying, recording, scanning, or otherwise without written permission from the publisher. It is illegal to copy this book, post it to a website, or distribute it by any other means without permission. Estelle Rose asserts the moral right to be identified as the author of this work.

This book is copyright protected. This book is only for personal use. You cannot amend, distribute, sell, use, quote or paraphrase any part, or the content within this book, without the consent of the author or publisher.

Under no circumstances will any blame or legal responsibility be held against the publisher, or author, for any damages, reparation, or monetary loss due to the information contained within this book. Either directly or indirectly. You are responsible for your own choices, actions, and results.

Designations used by companies to distinguish their products are often claimed as trademarks. All brand names and product names used in this book and on its cover are trade names, service marks, trademarks and registered trademarks of their respective owners. The publishers and the book are not associated with any product or vendor mentioned in this book. None of the companies referenced within the book have endorsed the book.

Please note the information contained within this document is for educational and entertainment purposes only. All effort has been executed to present accurate, up to date, and reliable, complete information. No warranties of any kind are declared or implied. Readers acknowledge that the author is not engaging in the rendering of legal, financial, medical or professional advice. The content within this book has been derived from various sources. Please consult a licensed professional before attempting any techniques outlined in this book.

By reading this document, the reader agrees that under no circumstances is the author responsible for any losses, direct or indirect, which are incurred as a result of the use of the information contained within this document, including, but not limited to, — errors, omissions, or inaccuracies.

First edition

contents

Introduction	xi
How To Use This Book	xv

WEEK 1: GETTING STARTED — 1

1. **ADHD AND ORGANIZATION** — 3
   Why Are We So Messy While Craving Organization?
2. **WHY OVER HOW** — 13
   Change Your Relationship with Organization for Good

WEEK 2: DESIGN A HOME THAT WORKS FOR YOU — 27

3. **ADHD MINIMALISM** — 29
   Own Less, Stress Less, and Create a Clutter-Proof Life
4. **MAKE IT MAKE SENSE** — 41
   Design a Space That Supports Your ADHD Life

WEEK 3: BUILDING MOMENTUM — 59

5. **THE ART OF FOLLOWING THROUGH** — 61
   How to Make Maintenance Effortless
6. **TIDYING UP WITH OTHERS** — 73
   (and Yes, Children Too)
7. **DEBUGGING YOUR LIFE** — 85
   How to Build Systems That Can Bend Without Breaking

WEEK 4: AROUND THE HOUSE — 93

8. **MAKING YOUR KITCHEN ADHD-FRIENDLY** — 95
   Create a Space for Nourishment and Sanity
9. **BATHROOM WITH A CAUSE** — 103
   Less Guilt, More Glow
10. **REST IS NOT A LUXURY** — 111
    Design a Bedroom That Helps You Sleep Better and Think More Clearly
11. **DRESSED WITHOUT STRESS** — 119
    Kill the Decision Fatigue, and Finally Find Your Pants
12. **A WORKING WORKSPACE** — 131
    How to Create a Productive Environment (Digitally and In Real Life)

IN CONCLUSION	147
Also by Estelle Rose	151
About the Author	154
Bibliography	155

*To all my fellow humans who find the world
too loud and too dark.
You're not alone.*

introduction

It started with a playdate.

Or, more accurately, a full-blown, shame-fueled panic attack over a playdate.

A new friend had texted to say she was on her way over with her kids, and I immediately felt my stomach drop.

I looked around my living room, and it was a disaster zone. Not just a little untidy. It was like a tornado had thrown a tantrum in it. Toys were everywhere, forgotten snack plates littering the coffee table, a pile of laundry I'd been meaning to "deal with" for a couple of weeks, and at least two cups of cold coffee that had been abandoned mid-task. And that was just the living room.

The kitchen? That was a certified crime scene. Dishes stacked high in the sink, counters covered in random clutter, and a vague but distinct smell of something that should have been thrown out days ago.

I felt a wave of shame so strong that it practically knocked the air out of my lungs.

I did not want this new mom-friend to see my house like this. So, I did what any self-respecting ADHD-er in panic mode does: I freaked out and launched into frantic, adrenaline-fueled speed cleaning. I shoved things into closets, threw dishes into the dishwasher (even though there was a clean half-load left in there), and did that thing where you just move mess from one room to another, creating a slightly more contained mess.

By the time she arrived, the place was still a mess, but at least you could walk to the laundry-free couch without breaking a toy. I was out of breath and on the verge of a stress meltdown.

And after that? For months, I didn't invite anyone over.

Instead of dealing with the mess, I hid from it. I stopped making plans. I dreaded stepping into my kitchen every morning as returning to piles of dishes and papers, with half-consumed food thrown in the mix, made me feel like I was failing at adulthood.

Little did I know that I was in good company: 77% of adults with ADHD struggle with organization in daily life. It's not me saying it; it's a 2020 Canadian study. The struggle with organization runs deep: it affects our work, our relationships, and most importantly, our own sense of peace and self-worth.

It's not just about losing your keys for the hundredth time or having a chairdrobe that's more of a clothing mountain than an actual place to sit. It's about the constant, underlying stress of knowing you need to get organized but feeling paralyzed about where to start, no matter how many times we promise ourselves we'll "get it together."

But here's the thing: It's not that we don't know what to do. We've read the books, saved the checklists, maybe even created a Pinterest board or binged a few too many home organization shows and YouTube shorts, fantasizing about a life where everything is neatly color-coded.

The problem isn't the knowing; it's the doing. That same 2020 Canadian study (a.k.a. Durand study) "supports that individuals with ADHD can efficiently develop strategies, but may have difficulties using those strategies in a continuous manner."

No kidding!

Would you agree we "have difficulties"
following through and getting things done?

Well, yeah, Estelle! Duh! That's why I've picked
this book in the first place.

I thought so. And that's where this book swoops in with a shiny armour to save the day. Forget the rigid, one-size-fits-all system you try for a week before abandoning completely. Not on my watch!

I've created a 28-day framework designed specifically for ADHD brains: I will walk you step by step through creating a space that works for you, not against you.

And yes, even if you're totally overwhelmed and don't know where to start.

Why 28 days? Because anything shorter would be a joke and send you on another cleaning binge, only to leave you exhausted and let the clutter creep back in no time.

I'm here for the long haul. Are you?

A 28-day framework gives you just enough structure to get started and build momentum. I've broken things down into manageable chunks to help you build routines that stick. By the time we're done, you won't just have an organized space, you'll have a system that you can actually maintain.

> But why should I listen to you, Estelle?
>
> You're quite a mess yourself, by the sound of it.

> Well, it takes one to know one!
>
> But true, I used to be. Let me finish my story.

After a few months of hibernating, I realized the problem wasn't just that my home was messy. It was that my brain was trapped in a constant state of chaos because of it.

Now, let's get one thing straight. If you're looking for a book to help you create a magazine-spread-worthy home, this is not that book.

But if, like me, waking up to a disaster every morning makes you feel exhausted before the day has even started, keep reading and you'll find a practical, long-lasting, ADHD-friendly approach to organization: one that helps you create living and working spaces that support your brain and the life you want.

To be totally transparent: as I'm writing this book, if you walked into my living room, you would find a remote control left on the couch, my kids' homework scattered across the coffee table, and at least one pair of headphones on the sofa. It's definitely a lived-in house. So, indeed, you might be asking yourself, "Who on earth are you to share advice on organizing and cleaning?"

Well, I'm a woman with ADHD who knows what it's like to feel completely overwhelmed by the mess and to step out of it, for good. I'm also a productivity coach and the author of a few books on ADHD, including *The Empowering ADHD Workbook for Women* and *Adult ADHD Executive Function 7-Week Power Up*. So, at the risk of bragging, I know a thing or two about helping fellow adults with ADHD.

Imagine coming back to a home that calms you down after an exhausting day. Imagine waking up every morning to a home that boosts your mood, gives you clarity, and sends you off on a productive day. And imagine maintaining it in a way that feels right to you and the people you live with, whatever your circumstances.

My house is far from spotless, but you know what? It's better: It's functional. It's a space where I can work, my family can live, and my brain can feel calmer. I can make my morning coffee without having to clear a path first. My kids can do their homework at the kitchen table because there's actually room for them to do it, and I can invite you over for tea without spiraling into shame-induced panic cleaning.

So, if you're ready to break free from the chaos, finally put an end to the shame spiral of ADHD organization struggles, and create a home that helps you feel calmer and more productive, let's get started.

how to use this book

DISCLAIMER

You probably don't expect to find medical advice in a book about organization and cleaning. But just in case, I just want to be very clear that I am not a psychiatrist and this is not medical advice. I'm a fellow ADHDer and coach who's done the research so you don't have to. I'm here to share my experience and cheer you on.

HOW TO READ THIS BOOK

Each week, you'll find a few chapters to read, followed by daily tasks to make sure you implement them straight away. There are also extra journaling prompts to download if you're keen on deeper work.

You can read this book as intended, one week at a time. Or you can binge-read it all first, then go through the 28-day framework while re-reading the relevant chapters (or key takeaways.

If you need more time, or if there is a day when you can't do the daily tasks, that's absolutely fine. You can pause for a day and come back to it. You will quickly understand the spirit in which the 28-day workbook is written. Just keep coming back.

WORKBOOK

To make the most out of this novel, I've prepared a downloadable workbook for you. You'll find all of the daily tasks, with extra space to write and extra journaling prompts to help your transformation.

You can print it if you want, or use the Google Docs version to be able to fill it in there and then. You'll just have to create your own copy. Grab it here: linke.to/organization

BEFORE YOU START

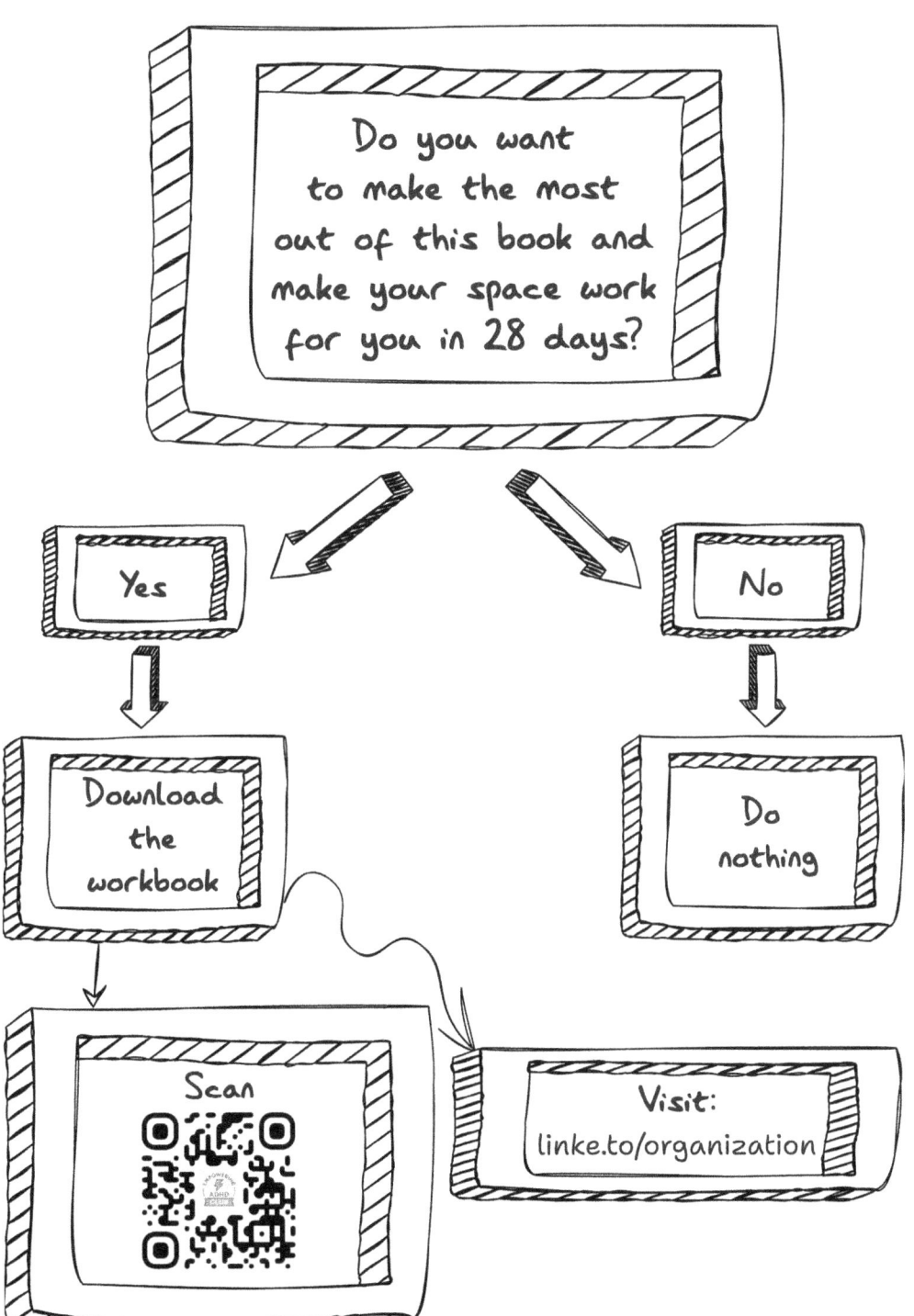

week 1: getting started

CHAPTER ONE
adhd and organization
WHY ARE WE SO MESSY WHILE CRAVING ORGANIZATION?

No matter which angle you take: neurological, psychological, or my personal favorite, biosocial (which looks at both biological predispositions and environmental factors), everything points in the same direction. ADHD and disorganization go hand in hand.

It's almost laughable how consistent this pattern is. The Durand study tells us that people with ADHD are 2.5 times more likely to struggle with maintaining an organized workspace. That's not just an annoying little quirk: it can get in the way of our careers, relationships, mental health, and ability to function day-to-day.

So, let's start by taking a look at what is at play here. Don't worry; I'm not going to turn this into a lecture in biochemistry, but understanding why we do things is always the first step toward change.

1. WHY WE'RE MESSY: THE NEUROLOGICAL CULPRITS

Executive Dysfunction

There's increasing evidence that executive dysfunction is one of the biggest challenges for adults with ADHD. If you want to dive deeper into this, you can read my previous book, *Adult ADHD Executive Dysfunction 7-Week Power-Up*, but for now, let's break it down simply.

Executive function is essentially the brain's command center. It handles planning, prioritization, time management, impulse control, and working memory: all the skills that help people stay organized and on top of daily life. So, messiness and lack of organization are not flaws; they're the direct result of executive dysfunction.

"Where Did I Put That?"

If you've ever put something down and forgotten where you placed it two seconds later, that's your working memory deficit in action. The same goes when you start tidying up, but halfway through, you're suddenly standing in the middle of a room, holding an empty mug, and can't remember why.

That's because our brains struggle to hold and manipulate multiple pieces of information simultaneously. So, multi-step tasks can feel impossible. Our struggle with working memory is also related to our "out of sight, out of mind" signature move: if we can't see an object, it might as well not exist.

"Where Should I Start?"

When we walk into a cluttered space, everything demands attention at the same time, we see a million tiny, interconnected decisions, and that's when task paralysis kicks in. Our brain simply can't decide where to start.

Should I start with the dishes? Wait, there are papers on the counter, maybe I should file those? But before I do that, I need to find a pen. What would be the best pen for the job? Where are my 'good pens? And suddenly, we're elbows-deep in a junk drawer, rediscovering old receipts from five years ago.

Our brains struggle to rank tasks in order of importance, which leads to complete overwhelm, so we just decide to deal with it ~~never~~ "later". But more on that in a second.

That's when the 28-day framework comes to the rescue, and I'll show you the simplest prioritisation matrix that works every time to get you out of your procrastination station.

"I'll Do It Later" (Spoiler: You Won't)

Time blindness makes things even trickier. If we needed any proof, another 2020 study published in *Applied Neuropsychology* found that

"Adults with ADHD had more problems in their daily life, especially with regard to time management and completing daily chores."

Our brains don't sense the passage of time in the same way neurotypical brains do, which is another reason to put things off. We also either drastically underestimate or wildly overestimate how long something will take.

We tell ourselves that washing the dishes will only take five minutes, only to realize it's a much bigger job, and now we don't have the time or energy. Or, we convince ourselves that cleaning the kitchen will take forever, so we put it off, when it would have taken just ten minutes, and make our whole day feel more productive.

Throw hyperfocus in the mix: we get so absorbed in everything other than cleaning that we completely lose track of time, and "later" becomes "never."

"Let Me Google Take Real Quick"

Imagine you start decluttering your desk, and then you find a rubber duck: a thoughtful gift from a secret Santa. Instead of releasing it into the world of second-hand delights or adding it to your collection on your bathtub, your brain goes:

When were rubber ducks invented? Let me Google that real quick. Oh wow, the history of bath toys is fascinating. Wait, what was I doing again?

And just like that, cleaning derails you into a deep dive of random knowledge.

ADHD impulsivity means we struggle to stay on task, and when combined with hyperfocus, it can lead to projects being started but never finished.

Beyond Executive Dysfunction

In addition to executive dysfunction, one of the biggest culprits is our infamous dopamine deficiency. In case you've never come across it, dopamine is the neurotransmitter responsible for motivation, reward, and focus. And ADHD brains don't produce enough of it.

Now, let's face it: cleaning and organizing can feel mundane and repetitive, meaning we'd rather do anything else. But fear not, we'll learn how to change that and turn organizing into a dopamine machine. Okay, that might be a slightly hyped exaggeration, but I'll definitely share hacks that make it feel more rewarding. Let's examine the other factors that contribute to our messiness first.

If your space is a constant state of chaos, it's not because you're lazy. It's not because you don't care. I know, you know, we both know. But sometimes the world around us tells us a different story, and guess what? That story is not helpful.

2. THE SOCIAL AND PSYCHOLOGICAL REASONS BEHIND ADHD MESSINESS

As if executive dysfunction and dopamine deficiency were not enough, organization (or the lack of it) is also profoundly shaped by our past experiences, social conditioning, emotional regulation, and cultural expectations.

Learned Helplessness

Have you spent your whole life hearing about how messy, forgetful, or disorganized you are? Did your parents make exasperated remarks about your inability to keep your room tidy? Maybe even now, as an adult, your partner, friends, or colleagues joke about how chaotic you are, reinforcing the idea that you are just *bad at this* and always will be.

Over time, all of that external criticism becomes internalized. When you hear something enough times, you start to believe it and feel like there's no point in trying at all. This is called learned helplessness; it keeps us stuck, and it's incredibly common in adults with ADHD.

It's not just that we *struggle* to stay organized; it's that, deep down, many of us believe we *can't* be organized ever.

Learned Disorganization

There's also a possibility that you never had the chance to learn organization in the first place. If you grew up in a home where organization wasn't modeled or reinforced, you might never have developed the skills or habits needed to maintain an organized space.

If you didn't have clear expectations, routines, and consequences, or if you grew up in a home where clutter is the norm, where cleaning happens in bursts of frantic energy rather than as a consistent habit, while being yelled at for doing it wrong, of course it's going to feel impossible now.

The good news? Just because you didn't learn these skills in childhood doesn't mean you can't learn them now.

And if you have kids, I can see you turning pale with parental guilt. Stop right here. It's not too late. You've picked up this book, you're ready for change, and modeling organizational skills to your children might just be the motivation you need for the long haul. Plus, I've got you covered: we'll discuss organizing with children in week 3.

The Emotional Weight of Mess

Mess isn't just about stuff: it's about emotions. Our struggles with organization are often deeply tied to feelings of failure, shame, and stress.

When we look at a chaotic space, we don't just see a mess; we see evidence of our own inadequacies. We remember every time we've failed to get our life together, every moment of frustration, every comment from someone who made us feel like we weren't trying hard enough.

The shame can be paralyzing. It can keep us from inviting people over, asking for help, or even attempting to make changes.

And for women with ADHD, this weight is even heavier. Culturally, we are expected to be naturally organized, capable of juggling everything: acing work, raising children, keeping a spotless home, and somehow making it all look effortless. But that's not realistic for anyone, ADHD or not. And yet, those expectations are still deeply rooted, making the struggle with organization feel even more like a personal failing rather than what it really is: a difference in how our brains work.

Social Norms

Social norms around organization are often rigid and inaccessible to ADHD brains.

We're told to follow strict processes, use detailed checklists, and "just be more disciplined." But those traditional approaches often feel suffocating. That's why I prefer to help you create your own system: the one that works for you.

That rigid perfection also contributes to procrastination. If we believe that an organized space means flawless, Pinterest-perfect minimalism, the task feels so overwhelming that we might as well not start. If we can't do it *perfectly*, then why bother doing it at all?

So, some of us decide to rebel against those norms. At some point, instead of trying (and failing) to be "better," we lean into it. We adopt the identity of the messy, chaotic, but maybe creative and quirky, and wear it like a badge of honor. Who cares if my place is a disaster? That just means I'm free-spirited! I'm too busy with an interesting life to worry about vacuuming!

And if that works for you and you're happy, go for it. Stop reading now and embrace the mess. But you've picked this book, so I'm going to guess that mess is bothering you. So, let's look at why that might be the case and what an organized space can do for us.

3. WHY WE NEED AN ORGANIZED SPACE

By now, we've established two key things: First, struggling with organization is not a character flaw. And second, the goal of getting organized is not about conforming to society's rigid expectations. We are doing this because our external environment has a direct impact on our internal world. But how?

Sensory Overload

ADHD and sensory sensitivities often go hand in hand. While neurotypical brains might filter out background noise, visual clutter, or other distractions, ADHD brains struggle to do so.

Our brains are constantly taking in information, whether we want them to or not. A messy room isn't just a messy room: it's a bombardment of stimuli that our brains have to process. Every pile, every misplaced object, every unfinished task sitting in plain sight is like a blinking neon sign screaming for attention.

This sensory overload is exhausting. When your brain constantly works overtime to process everything at once, it drains your energy fast. And the more drained we feel, the less energy we have to actually do anything about the mess.

So we push it to the back of our minds, ignore it, pretend it doesn't exist, until one day, it's become so overwhelming that we can't avoid it anymore.

Mess-Stress-Executive Dysfunction Cycle

Mess actively impacts our mental and emotional well-being. It can trigger anxiety, make it harder to focus, and interfere with our ability to concentrate, work, study, or even relax.

ADHD brains are already prone to elevated levels of cortisol, the stress hormone. When we're surrounded by mess, our cortisol levels rise even more.

The more stressed we feel, the more intense our ADHD symptoms become, executive dysfunction worsens, decision paralysis kicks in, and motivation plummets. And that makes it even harder to do something about the mess, which, in turn, makes us more stressed. This is the mess-stress-executive dysfunction cycle, and it's a brutal loop to be stuck in.

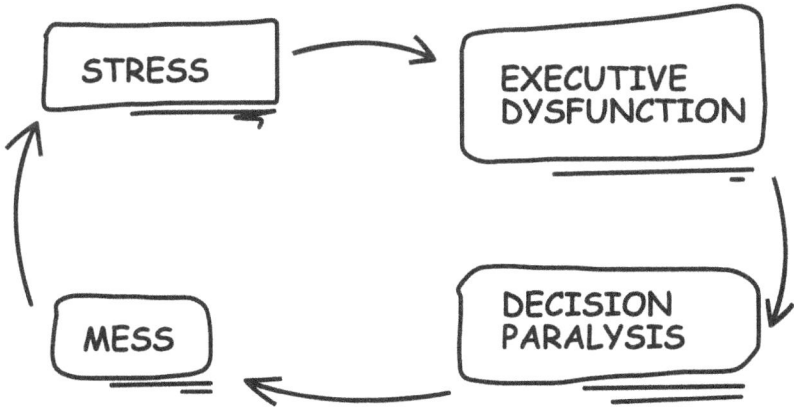

A 2016 UCLA study published in the journal *Social Science and Medicine* examined adults with ADHD and found that "certain environments amplified these difficulties, others seemed to make them disappear." The conclusion? People with ADHD aren't just sensitive to their environment; "their symptoms could be mitigated by selecting environments that were a good 'fit'."

In other words, a decluttered or ADHD-friendly space doesn't just prevent our symptoms from getting worse: it helps manage them.

FINAL THOUGHTS

An organized space can help us feel calmer, think more clearly, and function better. Which is precisely why I wrote this book.

Keep this between us, but I've spent years resisting writing a book on ADHD and organization. Mainly because I mostly work with women with ADHD, and the last thing I wanted was to contribute to the stereotype that women should be naturally interested in swapping tips about housework.

But here's the thing: I have seen time and time again, with almost every ADHD client I've ever worked with, that space had an enormous impact on how we feel, how we manage our symptoms, and how we move through the world.

So I thought it was time to dedicate a whole book to it. Because ADHD-friendly organization isn't just about decluttering: it's about creating a supportive environment that reduces stress, minimizes overwhelm, and helps us function at our best.

KEY TAKEAWAYS

- **Mess isn't a moral failing, it's neurological:** ADHD isn't just about being forgetful or distracted every now and then, it's a constant struggle with a brain that struggles to prioritize, remember, and manage time in a way that lines up with the world's expectations; a.k.a. executive dysfunction. If your home is a mess, it's not a reflection of your character: it's a reflection of how your brain processes the world. Also, low dopamine makes boring tasks feel even more boring.
- **Executive dysfunction makes organizing feel impossible:** Disorganization is often rooted in executive dysfunction. Your working memory makes it hard to keep track of what you're doing in the moment, especially when tasks have multiple steps. Your brain wants to do everything at once and ends up doing… nothing. Add in time blindness, impulsivity, and

ADHD's love affair with novelty, and tidying up never gets done.
- **Our past plays a role too:** If you grew up with constant criticism about being messy or never learned organizational skills in the first place, it makes sense that you struggle now. It's just unlearned (or wrongly learned) behaviour that we can absolutely rewrite.
- **Mess carries emotional weight**: Shame, guilt, fear of judgment. Especially for women, who are still expected to juggle careers, children, and spotless homes like it's a casual Tuesday. But spoiler alert: none of that expectation is fair or sustainable. The shame is heavy, but it doesn't belong to you.
- **It's a vicious loop**: Mess makes stress worse, and stress makes mess worse. Clutter overwhelms us, raises our stress levels, which worsens our ADHD symptoms, which makes it harder to organize, which creates more clutter. Rinse, repeat.
- **A supportive environment helps manage ADHD symptoms:** This book isn't about becoming a better housekeeper. It's about creating a space that supports your brain, so you can function better, think more clearly, and live more peacefully. It's not about impressing anyone. It's about feeling better in your space, your body, and your mind.

CHAPTER TWO

why over how

CHANGE YOUR RELATIONSHIP WITH ORGANIZATION FOR GOOD

IF WE WANT to banish clutter overload and task paralysis for good, we have to start in the right place. And no, that place is not your overflowing junk drawer or the laundry pile that's basically a piece of modern art at this point. We're starting with something far more important: acceptance.

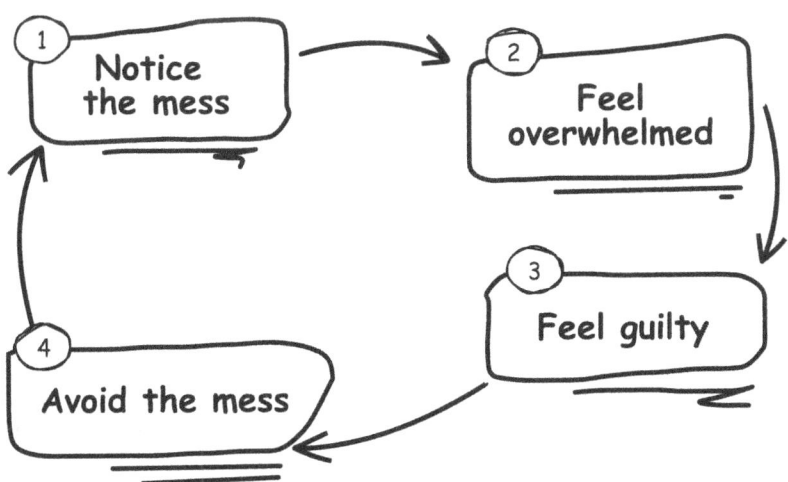

Because if we don't first work on our relationship with organization and tidying, we're heading straight into the same cycle of mess, overwhelm, guilt, and avoidance over and over again. And frankly, we have done it enough times, am I right?

So, before we even think about creating a system, we must let go of shame, guilt, and unrealistic expectations. We need to rewrite the stories we tell ourselves about mess and tidiness. And we need to accept a few fundamental truths that will make this entire process easier, kinder, and actually sustainable.

1. FOUR TRUTHS TO ACCEPT

Truth #1: Mess Is Not a Moral Failing

Hopefully, this one has already sunk in by now, but let's get this straight once and for all: being messy does not make you a bad person. And on the flip side? Being tidy doesn't make someone a better, more worthy human being. There is no moral superiority in being organized. You are not a more valuable person because your spice jars are alphabetized or your books arranged by spine color.

So let's reframe organization for what it really is: a form of self-care. Just something we're doing to make our lives easier and look after ourselves.

Systems Should Serve You, Not the Other Way Around

Raise your hand if you've ever bought a fancy planner or downloaded a 'perfect' checklist, only to abandon it within a week and feel like an absolute failure.

Spoiler alert: You're not the failure. The system failed you.

If a tool, strategy, or method doesn't actually help you, it doesn't belong in your life. It's not sacred. It's not a test of your worth. It's just a tool. If it's useful, keep it. If it's not, throw it out.

And that goes for every strategy in this book, too. These methods are not here to shame you or to be added to your growing 'must-do' list. If one works? Amazing. If one doesn't? That's the system's problem, not yours.

Truth #2: Function Beats Perfection

Perfectionism is the enemy of progress. We're not aiming for Pinterest perfection. We are aiming for functionality.

A space that works for you. A home where you can actually find your keys. A kitchen that makes you want to cook brain-boosting food. A level of organization that makes your life easier, not harder.

Progress over perfection

We also need to accept that this is an ongoing journey, and if I had a magic wand to clear your home in a day, I would use it, promise. Writing this book is the next best thing!

Even years in, my home is far from perfect. Sure, people can come over without me feeling like I need to stage an emergency clean-up operation. You can sit in my kitchen while I cook, and it won't be a disaster. But is it perfect? Absolutely not. Do you want to know how often I clean my windows? ~~Some things are better left unsaid.~~ I wouldn't want to overshare.

Progress beats perfection. Every. Single. Time. And I'll tell you this: if you go through the 28-day framework in this book, you will see progress. Even if you do it imperfectly (that's the spirit). Even if you skip days. Even if you don't go through the whole decluttering challenge. Even if you just pick and choose what works for you.

And the best part? Progress compounds. If you focus on getting just 1% better every day, by the end of the year, you'll be 37 times better. Yes, really. And I don't know about you, but I'm absolutely on board for that.

Stop Comparing Yourself to People Who Don't Have Your Brain

You might have heard that "to compare is to despair," and one of the fastest ways to kill your motivation is to compare yourself to people who do not have ADHD. Or worse, to some influencer's carefully curated, perfectly staged version of reality.

You do not have their brain. You do not have their circumstances. You have no idea what's outside the frame of that TikTok video. And if looking at those images makes you feel like a failure, unfollow, mute, step away.

The only person you should be measuring yourself against is Past You. And if today's *you* is even slightly more functional than last month's *you*? That's a win.

Truth #3: Accept the Cards You've Been Dealt

You have the space you have. You live with the people you live with. You have the time, energy, and resources that you have.

Wishing things were different won't change them. Complaining about how much work it takes won't make it easier. The sooner we accept our reality, the sooner we can start working with what we've got.

Whether you live in a tiny apartment or a massive house, have a supportive partner or one who "doesn't see mess," have kids running around or a chaotic work schedule that eats up your time, they all have pros and cons. This book will help you figure out a way to make it work.

Truth #4: How You Talk to Yourself Matters

Language is powerful.

If the phrase "tidy up" makes you instantly feel stressed, reframe it. I stopped calling it "tidying up" and "cleaning" long ago. Now, I call it a "reset". Because I'm not scrubbing away my sins, I'm just restoring my space to a version that makes my life easier.

And another thing worth keeping in mind: if you're catching yourself saying things like "I'm such a slob/idiot/failure," stop right now and rephrase with compassion, "My brain finds this challenging, but I'm creating systems that support me."

Here are 10 more examples of rephrasing that can help:

1. "I have to do the dishes." → "I get to wash the dishes."
2. "I can't do this." → "How can I do this?"
3. "I will never be able to do this." → "I can't do this yet."
4. "This is too hard for me." → "This is challenging."
5. "I'm not good at this." → "I can improve with practice."
6. "It's not worth trying if I might fail." → "Failure is part of learning."
7. "I'm too far behind to catch up." → "Progress happens one step at a time."

8. "I have no self-discipline." → "I can build better systems."
9. "I should be better at this by now." → "Progress isn't linear."
10. "I'm too overwhelmed to start." → "What's one small step I can take right now?"

From now on, celebrate every step forward and congratulate yourself. Did you manage to clear off one surface today? Amazing. Did you throw out one thing? Huge win. Did you do absolutely nothing except rest? Congratulations, you prioritized your well-being.

Because this time, we're not just trying to get organized. We're changing how we think about organization. And that's what will make the difference.

2. SETTING GOALS... THE ADHD WAY

If we really want to nail this whole transformation thing and truly change the way we think about organization, we need to make sure that whatever system we create is something we can actually sustain. That means we need goals. But not just any goals.

There's a lot of productivity advice floating around out there, and a whole lot of it is entirely incompatible with the ADHD brain. It sets us up for failure, increases burnout, and leaves us feeling like we just don't have what it takes to "get it together." If you're interested in productivity beyond tidying up, check my *Productivity Without Pressure* training, it's all about that!

> Stop digressing, Estelle!
>
> But I love to nerd out on productivity.
>
> Sure, but we're here to organize and clean.
>
> Oh, yeah, let's go!

So we're going to approach this differently, as nothing kills motivation faster than a constant focus on everything we're failing at, rather than what we're capable of.

We've already established that the purpose is *not* to have a spotless home that would pass a magazine shoot test, but for ourselves, so that our space supports us, rather than conspires against us. So, let's grab our inner magnifying glass and look for internal validation.

Intrinsic Motivation vs Extrinsic Motivation

Extrinsic motivation consists of the outside forces that try to keep us on track. Think checklists, schedules, reminders, alarms, and accountability buddies. And don't get me wrong, these can be amazing tools, but they won't carry us through the long haul. Because when we're having one of those days, when we're exhausted, overwhelmed, and barely holding it together, a checklist is not going to get us off the couch magically.

What will? Intrinsic motivation. The internal drive that comes from us. And if you have ADHD, you know that intrinsic motivation can be slippery. That's why we need to anchor it. We need to drill down and make our "why" so clear, so profoundly personal, that it will still be there even when the external motivation runs out.

We've already covered the broad why: we want a space that helps us function better and make daily life easier. But we need to take it deeper than that. That's where the "Five Whys" come in (spoiler alert: you'll have to do it on day 4).

The Five Whys: Finding Your Real Motivation

You start with a simple question: Why do I want an organized space? And whatever answer you give, you ask why again, five times.

For example:

- *Why do I want an organized space?* → So I can feel less stressed at home.
- *Why do I want to feel less stressed at home?* → Because when my space is messy, I feel overwhelmed and exhausted.
- *Why do I want to stop feeling overwhelmed and exhausted?* → Because when I feel like that, I shut down and don't get anything done.
- *Why does that matter?* → Because I feel guilty when I don't get anything done, and it affects my confidence.
- *Why does that matter?* → Because I want to feel in control of my life, not constantly behind and drowning in chaos.

And there it is. The real motivation. Not just "I want a tidy space," but "I want to feel in control of my life." That's the kind of reason that keeps you going even when motivation is low.

Focus on What You Can Control

When we set goals, we tend to fixate on the end result: a spotless house, a perfectly organized workspace, a kitchen so pristine you could picnic on the floor without a blanket. But the problem is, those end results are not always entirely in our control and can feel overwhelming when we don't know where to start.

What we can control are the steps we take to get there.

For example, instead of setting a goal like *"I want an organized home,"* reframe it into something actionable. What is one small thing you can do to move toward that?

Maybe it's clearing your bedside table so that you don't immediately feel stressed out by clutter when you wake up. Maybe it's making sure the kitchen counter is clear before bed so that your morning starts on a better note. These are things you can control. Focusing on them means you'll make progress, rather than feeling stuck staring at the overwhelming big picture.

Forget SMART, Go NICE

Now, if you've ever sat through a productivity workshop, you've probably heard about SMART goals: Specific, Measurable, Achievable, Relevant, and Time-bound. And if you're anything like me, you've probably tried to come up with something… anything… and failed.

SMART goals have never worked for me. They feel uninspiring and are an instant motivation killer. And for years, I thought that meant I was the problem.

But then I came across something else: NICE goals. Credit goes to Ali Abdaal's *Feel-Good Productivity* for this one.

NICE goals

NICE stands for:

- **Near-term** - The goal should be something that can happen soon, not some vague "one day" plan, not even at the end of the 28-day framework. Near-term goals will provide the quick wins we need to build that momentum.
- **Implementable** - It should be practical and not just an abstract aspiration, something you can take action on immediately or

very soon. That's also the ideal time to think about when you're going to implement it.
- **Controllable** - The outcome should depend on you, not external factors. This prevents frustration caused by external factors that could derail your progress.
- **Explicit** - It should be clear and simple, leaving no room for ambiguity.

Let's say your big goal is to create a calming home. That's great, but it's not immediately actionable. If we make it a NICE goal, it could look like this:

- **Near-term -** "Starting today and for the rest of the week."
- **Implementable -** "I will clear the laundry off my bed right now. Then, for maintenance, I will clear it every night before going to bed."
- **Controllable -** "I can do this in 5 minutes, with no outside factors stopping me."
- **Explicit -** "I am picking up laundry and putting it in the basket every night before bed."

Now, instead of a vague and overwhelming long-term goal, you have a concrete action step that is manageable, realistic, and doable.

FINAL THOUGHTS

Making it to the end of this chapter already counts as progress. Yes, really. Because you're not just reading words on a page. You're doing the brave, uncomfortable, and totally worthwhile work of shifting how you see yourself, your space, and the systems you live with.

The world is full of "how" advice. Organize like this. Follow this method. Try this trick. And sure, some of it works... *for other people.* But for those of us with ADHD, the "how" will never stick unless we're clear on our "why."

I'm talking about the messy, raw, gut-level kind of why. The kind that says, *I want to stop feeling ashamed every time someone knocks on the door.* Or, *I want to wake up and not feel immediately behind.* Or even just, *I want to stop crying in the kitchen because I can't find a clean spoon.* That kind of why is what carries us forward on the days motivation goes missing.

And here's the beautiful part: once you know your why, you don't have to chase perfection. You don't need to impress anyone. You just need to start where you are and take the next doable step. And if that next step is simply putting the socks in the laundry basket today instead of leaving them on the chair (you know the one), that's valid. That's enough.

The key to this whole thing is momentum. As we've established, ADHD brains thrive on dopamine, and nothing feeds dopamine like quick wins. That's why NICE goals work so well. Instead of feeling overwhelmed by a massive, long-term project, over the next 28 days, you will create a series of quick, achievable wins that keep you going.

It's time to take action.

This week, we're going to set the goals that will keep us fueled, set ourselves up for quick wins, and start talking to ourselves with self-compassion, all the while beginning to make progress on our space.

KEY TAKEAWAYS

- **Organization starts with acceptance**: Before you dive into cleaning or reorganizing your life, start by letting go of shame, guilt, and the unrealistic belief that mess equals moral failure. Being messy does not make you a bad person; your worth has nothing to do with your junk drawer. Organization is a form of self-care, not a badge of honor.
- **The system failed you, not the other way around**: If checklists, planners, or routines haven't worked for you, it's not because you're broken. It's because they weren't designed for your brain. Let go of the shame and let's build something that actually fits.
- **Progress always beats perfection:** Your house doesn't need to look Instagram-worthy. It just needs to work for you. A "good enough" system that supports your life will always beat a perfect one that burns you out. So, stop measuring your progress against people who don't have ADHD, or against filtered influencer posts. The only person you need to be competing with is the version of you from last week.
- **You've got to work with the life (and the laundry) you've got**: Your space, your people, your energy levels: these are the

fundamental building blocks of your system. Accepting this helps you finally start moving forward with what's possible.
- **Language matters**: Words like "lazy" and "should" have no place here. Reframe "tidy up" into a "reset," and swap "I'm a failure" for "my brain finds this hard, but I'm learning." Self-compassion is not optional: it's the secret sauce.
- **You need a why that comes from the gut**: The kind of why that shows up when motivation is hiding under a blanket. Not "I want a clean house," but "I want to feel calm in the morning" or "I want to stop crying over clutter." This is what keeps you moving, even on hard days.
- **Set goals that are NICE**: Forget rigid and uninspiring goals. ADHD-friendly goals should be Near-term, Implementable, Controllable, and Explicit, because we need doable action steps, and deliver quick wins to build momentum. Starting with small, easy actions creates that satisfying snowball effect that will fuel our dopamine.

week 1 tasks: setting goals and getting started

DAY 1

Guess what? Today, we're not going to touch a thing. We're going to make plans.

- Grab a notebook or download the workbook (you can do it here: linke.to/organization). Brainstorm all the areas you would like to improve in your house. Don't censor yourself at this stage, just brain dump all your ideas.
- Out of all the areas/rooms, think about the one that would have the most impact on your well-being: a clean kitchen where you can cook brain boosting meals and enjoy family time, a living room where you can wind down and invite friends, a bedroom where you can retreat, sleep peacefully and wake up to a calming room.
- Now, pick the area/room that will help you the most, and let's create some NICE goals (Near-term, Implementable, Controllable, and Explicit). Again, don't censor yourself at this stage; brain dump everything and remember to be mindful of the language you use. E.g. to get a clean kitchen, *I get to*: do the dishes every night, return dishes to cupboard every morning, wipe the table after dinner, sweep after dinner, return the spices to the spice cupboard after dinner, chuck any rotten vegetables and out of date food when I bring grocery in, etc.

That's enough for today. If you feel overwhelmed by your list, don't be. I'll help you prioritize.

DAY 2

- Grab those NICE goals from yesterday. Now, let's select the one that will become your daily High-Impact Task (HIT). Pick the one that will require minimum effort for maximum impact: e.g., no dishes in the sink when I wake up would improve my

mood. Clear tops would encourage me to cook healthier food and boost my brain and energy, etc.
- Now, go do it. For the rest of the week, you're going to focus just on this one small goal: doing this task daily.

Day 3

- If you haven't yet, plan *when* you're going to do your High-Impact Task (HIT). When are you most likely to do it? Set a reminder.
- Do whatever you need to do your HIT. E.g., wash those dishes, put those clothes in the laundry basket, etc.

Day 4

- Now, let's set up your *why*, the one that will keep you going. Drill down 5 times on why you want an organized/clean home, just like we've seen in Chapter 2.
- Do your High-Impact Task (HIT) while timing yourself. Was it under 5 minutes? If it's taking you more, maybe you're being too ambitious and need to break it down further.

Day 5

- Broadly assess the cards you are dealt with: Space, time, support.
- Let's gather intel by taking a tour around your space. Whether that's a box room or a mansion, it can only contain a certain amount. Accept this fact and walk around like a forensic inspector, jotting down places where you have too much stuff. Think overflowing wardrobes and spice racks. Make a note of it, we'll use the intel next week.
- Do your High-Impact Task (HIT).

Day 6

- Do your HIT. As you do, consider the following:
- How do you talk to yourself when it comes to organization?
- What wins can you already celebrate this week?
- What is your organizing self-care intention? For example, I get to do the dishes to feel good about myself. Doing the dishes in

the evening only takes me 4 minutes, and it helps me feel positive in the morning.

DAY 7

- Do your High-Impact Task (HIT) and as you do, consider whether you'd like to add a complementary one. Perhaps you've already done so without realising. If you've kept your bed laundry-free, maybe you've started to tackle that pile on the floor, too, a.k.a. floordrobe.
- Check your NICE goals. Brain dump any new idea, and plan a new HIT to add to your current one. Remember: minimum effort for maximum impact. If this room/area already feels functional, repeat the process in another room.
- Congratulate yourself for making a dent. The first step is the hardest.

week 2: design a home that works for you

CHAPTER THREE
adhd minimalism

OWN LESS, STRESS LESS, AND CREATE A CLUTTER-PROOF LIFE

WE KNOW from last week that taming the mess helps our brain perform better. Brilliant! But what if we could go even a step further? What if we could not just avoid making symptoms worse but actually make them better?

This week, we're going to look beyond tidying up and cleaning and introduce intentionality to start designing the space we need for the life we want. To help us along the way, we're going to look at a couple of design principles, starting with minimalism.

> What, now? You've just said it wasn't about creating a picture-perfect interior, Estelle, and now, you're all about minimalism?

> Don't worry. I haven't changed my mind about why we're tidying up. But for us folks with ADHD, minimalism can be our lifeline.

Here's the deal: our brains are already cluttered enough without our physical spaces adding to the chaos. Minimalism isn't just aesthetically pleasing, it's brain-pleasing. When I talk about minimalism for ADHD, I'm talking about a practical approach that acknowledges our unique neurology.

Think about it this way: owning less stuff equals managing less stuff.

Revolutionary concept, right? But for those of us whose executive function likes to go on unscheduled vacations, it's life-changing.

Minimalism helps us in three key ways:

1. **It reduces visual overwhelm** - Every item in our space is screaming for our attention. For our ADHD brains that struggle with filtering stimuli, fewer items mean fewer things competing for our already divided attention.
2. **It redirects our dopamine-seeking behavior** - Instead of chasing the temporary high of acquiring new things, we can find more sustainable sources of joy and satisfaction. This mindset helps us resist those 2 AM impulse avocado slicer purchases that seem absolutely essential in the moment.
3. **It is easier to maintain** - At its core, minimalism is just math: less stuff = less to clean = more time for literally anything else more interesting than cleaning.

So, you know what's coming right...? Decluttering. But this time, thanks to intentionality and simple concepts, we're not going to go through a humongous purge, only to re-clutter a few weeks later.

1. HOW TO DECLUTTER WHEN YOUR BRAIN FIGHTS YOU EVERY STEP OF THE WAY

So remember the cards we're dealt? And by cards, I mean the square footage of our homes. We need to apply this mindset to smaller units, too, sorry.

Working With What You've Got

Your closet has a finite capacity. Your kitchen cabinets can only hold so much. When these spaces are overflowing, it's not the space's fault; it's a sign we need to make some decisions.

And that's where the trouble starts, isn't it? Clutter isn't just stuff: it's a collection of unmade decisions. That shirt you never wear because you're not sure about it? Unmade decision. Those papers stacked on the kitchen counter that you might need someday? Unmade decisions. The six half-empty bottles of shampoo that get in the way of cleaning your bathroom? You guessed it.

For our ADHD brains, decision-making is particularly challenging because it relies heavily on executive function. And we know that's the very thing our brains struggle with most. But don't worry, I've got some techniques that can help make this process less overwhelming.

And if you suddenly get the urge to declutter (hello, hyperfocus!), don't fight it: ride that wave, my friend.

However, even amid a decluttering sprint, try to maintain some intentionality. Remember to start where it will have the maximum impact and what purpose your space serves, then make decisions accordingly.

Three Questions to Cut Through the Clutter

When you're face-to-face with an object and trying to decide its fate, ask yourself:

1. **"Does it spark joy?"** We have to quote the queen of decluttering here, of course. But the ADHD translation is: Do I love it? Does it give me a little dopamine hit?
2. **Do I need it?** Be honest: not "might need it someday."
3. **Do I actually use it?** As in, right now, ever? Not "plan to use it eventually"

If the answer to all three is no, then it's time to part ways, and we'll check how to do this just after looking at what to do with things that deserve to stay.

For items that pass the keep test, the next question is: "Does it have a home?" If yes, return it there. If not, we need to find one.

How to Find the Right Home for Your Stuff

When deciding where something should live, consider:

1. **Where do I use it?** Ideally, items should live where they're used.
2. **How often do I use it?** This determines how accessible it should be, a.k.a. In which tier do I put it?

Let's create a simple "tier system" for storing your belongings based on how often you use them:

Tier 1: "In Plain Sight" (Daily Use Items)

- **What goes here:** Things you use every single day
- **Examples:** Phone charger, medications, deodorant, keys
- **Where to store them:** Out in the open, visible, within arm's reach

See how it goes against those Instagram-perfect minimalist spaces? The trick is: we need to see things to remember they exist. So keep them visible without shame, and your brain will thank you!

Tier 2: "Easy Access" (Regular Use Items)

- **What goes here:** Things you use several times a week
- **Examples:** Extra toiletries, frequently worn clothing, cooking utensils
- **Where to store them:** In drawers, cabinets, or containers that require minimal effort to access

Tier 3: "Secondary Storage" (Occasional Use Items)

- **What goes here:** Things you use monthly
- **Examples:** Special occasion clothes, extra bedding, specific hobby supplies
- **Where to store them:** Closets, under-bed storage, higher shelves… but still accessible

Label these containers clearly! Future You will thank Past You for this small act of kindness.

Tier 4: "Deep Storage" (Rare Use Items)

- **What goes here:** Seasonal items or things with significant value used 1-2 times a year.
- **Examples:** Holiday decorations, seasonal clothing
- **Where to store them:** Attic, basement, back of closets, under beds

This is the danger zone! Items here often fall into the "out of sight, out of mind" abyss. I once rediscovered my extra winter coats in July in a suitcase when packing for the summer holidays. So, it is wise to:

1. **Set calendar reminders** to check your Tier 4 storage areas once per season
2. **Create a simple inventory** of what's in deep storage (even a photo on your phone added to that reminder)
3. **Reassess regularly,** an item may need to move to a different zone as your habits change

The perfect storage system isn't the prettiest one; it's the one you'll actually maintain and that helps you function better (hello, easier morning routine).

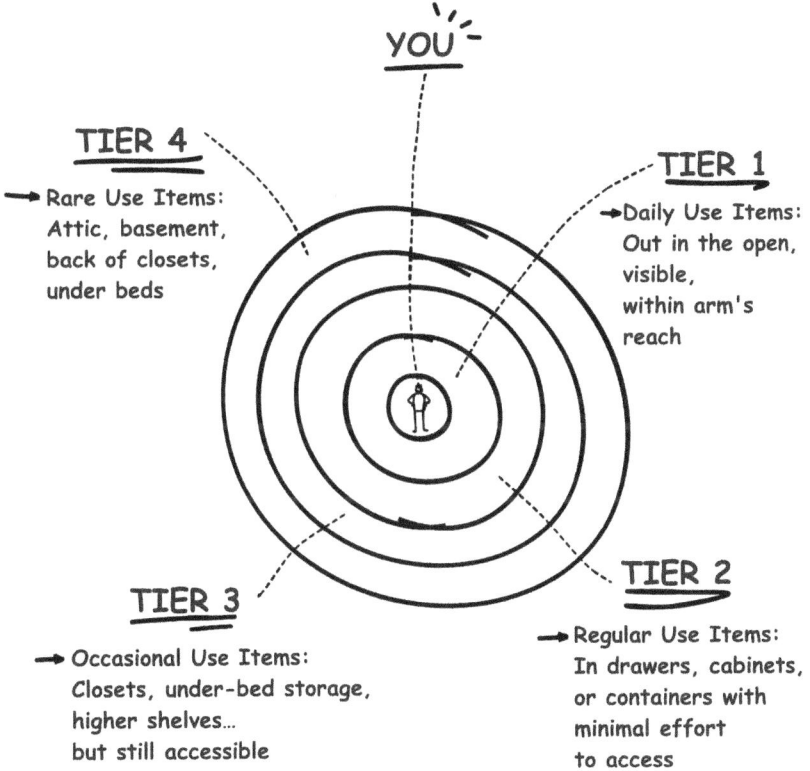

Letting Things Go

Once you've decided something needs to go, act quickly. The longer it sits in your "to donate" pile, the more likely it will migrate back into your "keep" pile through mysterious clutter physics.

33

Ask yourself: "Trash or donate?" Be realistic about the condition of items. That shirt with the mysterious stain will probably not make someone else's day.

> I know! I could sell it on Vinted, right Estelle!?

> Yes, but
>
> ...
>
> Is it really worth your time, though?

Now, I understand the appeal of making money from your castoffs. Who doesn't want to recoup some cash from that juicer you were convinced would change your life? But you need to be brutally honest with yourself.

Consider how long it will take to:

- Clean the item
- Take photos
- Write a listing
- Communicate with buyers
- Package and ship it
- Now, double that time estimate. Because, you know, ADHD.

So, the question is: Is the potential profit worth those hours of your life? Set a minimum value for items you'll sell. Maybe anything worth less than $10-20 automatically goes to donation. Your time is valuable, and your energy even more, even if your brain tries to tell you otherwise.

So, ready to donate? Here is how to get rid of your clutter quickly:

1. **Pick a place that takes everything** - You don't want offloading your clutter to turn into a two-hour round trip because you're donating books here, bric-a-brac there, and clothes in another place.
2. **Pick a place that is easy to access** - Ideally on a regular commute or close to you.
3. **Give yourself a deadline** - If you're on a long decluttering streak, make it part of your weekly routine and schedule a

regular drop. For now, I've got you covered and added a reminder to our 28-day framework.

2. WHEN MOTIVATION GOES MISSING

You bought this book, so you've probably got some sort of motivation to get organized right now.

But what about those days when even opening this book feels like too much effort? Trust me, I get it. Some days, the executive function fairy just doesn't show up for work, and the thought of making even one more decision feels like climbing Mount Everest in flip-flops.

Decluttering is not forever, but you don't have to tackle it all in one day either. Our ADHD brains often trick us into thinking everything must be done RIGHT NOW, but let's reframe that.

If your motivation is high, absolutely go for it! Ride that hyperfocus wave like the beautiful neurodivergent surfer you are. But once you're exhausted (and you will be), give yourself time. The clutter didn't appear overnight, and it doesn't need to disappear overnight.

Gamify Your Decluttering

Gamification can be a powerful tool for our ADHD brains. We're wired for novelty and challenge. When traditional organizing feels about as exciting as watching paint dry, turning it into a game can bypass that resistance and tap into our natural competitiveness (even if it's just competing with ourselves).

Here are some of my current favorites that I've seen work best:

The One-Thing-A-Day Method

A gentle approach is needed when life feels too much and your brain screams for mercy. Sometimes, the kindest thing you can do is start impossibly small. Like, ridiculously small. So small that your brain can't even be bothered to put up a fight. Here is how it works:

1. Each day, put just one thing in a designated "to donate" bag (or straight into the trash).
2. Put a reminder, ideally at some point in your daily routine, that will make it easier for you.

3. Do a weekly "getting rid of things" session with your collection.

The 21-Day Challenge

Not for the faint-hearted, but brilliant when a radical decluttering is needed.

Sometimes our ADHD brains need a little more spice in our organizational salsa. That's when a progressive challenge can be just the ticket: it starts manageable but builds enough momentum to keep our interest piqued.

1. Day 1: Remove one thing
2. Day 2: Remove two things
3. Day 3: Remove three things
4. And so on...

That's the one we'll be on for the next three weeks of our 28-day framework, which means you'll have removed 231 items by the end! If you're already quite minimalist, you can do it for just a week or pick another challenge, like one thing a day, or any of the ones below.

The Feng Shui Time Attack

If the thought of decluttering for hours makes you want to fake your own disappearance and start a new life in a different country, use a timer. The beauty of time-based challenges is that they have a clear beginning and end. You can do anything for five minutes, right? (Please say yes.)

1. Find nine items to get rid of in just five minutes
2. If you choose to do this for 21 days, you'd remove 189 items!

The 27 Fling Boogie

Another time-based challenge that can be a great addition to a weekly cleaning practice and keep decluttering long-term.

1. Get rid of 27 items in 15 minutes
2. It's basically a longer version of the Feng Shui Time Attack
3. If you did this weekly for the next three weeks, you'd remove 81 items

Call in Reinforcements

We're social creatures, after all, and sometimes the only thing that can get us moving is knowing someone else is watching (or doing it alongside us), so involving family and friends can help. A lot. It's like having a gym buddy, but for your closet.

Ask a friend if they're keen to play along. You don't even have to be in the same room. Just keep checking in with each other. Or, if you want to join a like-minded community of ADHDers who truly get the struggle, maybe it's time for you to join the Empowering ADHD Club. There's something powerfully motivating about knowing you're not the only one parting with eight out-of-date night creams you forgot you bought.

Maintaining Your Hard-Won Order

Once you've made a proper dent in decluttering, we want to prevent clutter creep. Here are five strategies to help:

1. **Question new acquisitions rigorously** - Do I really need it? Will I really use it? Does it genuinely spark joy? How will I feel about it next month, next year? Will it still spark joy?
2. **Decline freebies** - Free stuff isn't free if it costs you your peace of mind. And if you're thinking in terms of storage space, it's costing you money, too.
3. **Schedule your next decluttering session** while you're still feeling somewhat accomplished. Future You will probably try to talk yourself out of it, so make a date with your decluttering that's as non-negotiable as a dental appointment. Unless, of course, you're completely done, in which case, consider step four.
4. **Implement a "one in, one out" rule** - New shirt? Old shirt goes. New book? Time to part with one you've read (yes, even mine, if you're not going to refer to it).
5. **Consolidate** - Now that they're all gathered in your bathroom cupboard, this is when you discover you are the proud owner of 1,069 Band-Aids. (And yes, it's probably time to retire the Peppa Pig ones. Or the plain ones. You pick!)

If you're feeling a bit daunted about what comes next, let me just say this: you are not expected to become a minimalist monk by next Tuesday.

This isn't about stripping your life down to beige furniture and one spoon. This is about designing a space that supports your brilliant, complex, ADHD brain. A space that soothes instead of shouts. A space where you can find your keys and your calm.

FINAL THOUGHTS

We've talked about decluttering with intention, not just frantically chucking things into bags because the overwhelm finally got too loud to ignore. We've explored ways to make decision-making easier, even for a brain that treats every object like it's auditioning for sentimental value.

If you're already feeling behind because we haven't done a massive purge in week one… breathe. You are exactly where you need to be: aware, curious, and maybe even a little bit hopeful and excited. That's more than enough to begin.

Next up? We're going to keep building on that momentum and start shaping your environment to actually work with your brain and your routines (or lack thereof). Because ADHD-friendly living isn't about cleaning harder. It's about designing smarter.

KEY TAKEAWAY

- **Minimalism is about brain relief**: For ADHD brains, minimalism means fewer distractions, less overwhelm, and more mental clarity. It's not about looking good, it's about feeling better.
- **Decluttering is about what matters most**: Start where it will have the most impact and ask three questions to cut through the chaos: Do I love it? Do I need it? Do I use it? If it's a "no" to all three, then let it go.
- **Give everything a home** based on how often you use it: Visibility matters. Accessibility matters. Tier 1: Daily-use items are out in the open, within arm's reach. Tier 2: Weekly-use items are easy to access. Think drawers and cabinets. Tier 3: Occasional-use items are tucked away but reachable (on higher

shelves or further back). Tier 4: Rare-use items go into deep storage, but with an inventory of what is in there.
- **Getting rid of stuff**: Move quickly once you've decided to donate or ditch something. The longer it hangs around, the higher the chance it'll magically reattach itself to your life. Don't let "I might sell it one day" become a storage strategy. Unless it's worth more than your time, skip the guilt and donate. Your energy is precious.
- **Use gamification to trick your brain**: Whether it's a timer challenge, a 21-day count-up, or a weekly "27 Fling Boogie," turning decluttering into a mini game taps into ADHD's love for novelty and momentum.
- **Start impossibly small**: One object a day is 365 things in a year. That's a lot of brain space cleared.

CHAPTER FOUR

make it make sense

DESIGN A SPACE THAT SUPPORTS YOUR ADHD LIFE

THINK OF IT THIS WAY: removing clutter is like taking off shoes that have been pinching your feet all day: immediate relief. But designing your environment? That's like getting custom orthotics that not only stop the pain but actually make walking feel like you've got a personal massaging squad pampering your feet through each step. We're not just removing what hurts; we're adding what helps.

1. FUNCTION OVER FANTASY

Following minimalism, there is another key concept we must look at to help us along the way: Functionality. It is the very essence of what we're doing here.

> Yeah, Estelle, we get it. I'm not trying to create an Instagram-worthy home; I just want to find my keys without having a meltdown.

> Exactly! So glad we're on the same page!

Functionality and Decluttering

As you work through your chosen decluttering challenge (especially if you're going for one of the more intensive approaches), infuse functionality into your decision. For instance, try to keep multi-use objects and let go of single-use items.

That bread maker that's been sitting on your countertop gathering dust? You know, the one you bought during that pandemic bread-making phase that lasted exactly three loaves? Maybe it doesn't deserve such prime real estate, or maybe you can let it go entirely. When you do feel like making bread (approximately once every solar eclipse), you can make it in the oven almost as easily.

Let's circle back and deepen decluttering questions 2 and 3: Do I need it? Do I use it? If you're struggling to answer these or lean toward "I might some day," enquire further:

1. How often do I actually use this? For real, not in that parallel universe where you have infinite time and energy.
2. Could something else I already own serve the same function? Hint: an oven to bake bread.
3. Is the convenience worth the space it takes up? Yep, I'm still talking about you bread-maker, you're out.

It's not about living like a minimalist monk with three possessions and a serene expression (although, go for it, if you can sustain it). It's about making thoughtful choices that support how you actually live, rather than how you imagined you might live when you ordered that pasta maker at 2 AM after watching a cooking show.

When our environment is intentionally designed to support us, daily life becomes easier, our stress levels decrease, and we can focus our energy on what truly matters to us, instead of spending it all on trying to remember where we put our phone while we're talking on it.

So, let's take a closer look at intentionality.

Functionality and Intentionality

Why is intentionality so important? Well, brains are pretty magical when we give them direction. Yes, even ADHD brains.

Just by being aware of our intentions and thoughts, our wonderful brains start working toward them without us even realizing it. When you set an intention, even decisions about where that screwdriver should live will unconsciously align with your purpose.

Sounds a bit too woo-woo for you? I'm not talking about magically manifesting, I'm talking about stacks of behavioural research like the ones compiled in *Does Goal Pursuit Require Conscious Awareness?* published in *The Oxford Handbook of Human Motivation*.

In your daily tasks this week, we'll start applying it to organization.

2. YOUR BRAIN'S BEST FRIEND

We're now ready to discuss "zoning" and why it's an ADHD game-changer. And no, I don't mean arguing with your local city council. I'm talking about creating designated spaces for specific activities in your home.

Think of zoning as creating little departments in your life mall. You wouldn't expect to find swimsuits in the grocery section, right?

Remember the studies review from *The Oxford Handbook of Human Motivation*? It explains that some behaviors become automatic through repetition and that rewards in our environment can unconsciously push us toward certain behaviors.

As far as organization is concerned, when your space is set up correctly for a specific activity, your brain gets the message: "Oh, we're doing this now!" without you having to wage that internal battle to get started.

Zones to Consider

Here's a fairly exhaustive list of zones you might consider creating in your home. Emphasis on *consider*.

- **Work/Study/Admin Zone:** A dedicated space for focused work, studying, or administrative tasks like paying bills. This could be a home office, a corner of your bedroom, or your dining table at specific times.
- **Relaxation Zone:** A comfortable space specifically for unwinding (not sleeping)
- **Sleep Zone:** Ideally, your bed should be primarily for sleeping and intimacy (if in the mood), not working, eating, or doom-scrolling until 3 AM.
- **Dining Zone:** A place dedicated to meals, which helps create boundaries around eating and can prevent the "standing in

front of the open fridge eating cheese" phenomenon that many of us know too well. I could write a whole other book about eating, food, and ADHD, but… Oh, wait, I have! It's called *Brain Boosting Food for Women with ADHD,* if you're interested.

- **Cooking Zone:** A functional kitchen space organized to make brain-boosting meal preparation easier and more appealing than ordering takeout for the fifth time this week.
- **Social Zone:** An area designed for hosting friends and family, with seating arranged to facilitate conversation.
- **Fitness Zone:** A designated area for exercise, or just enough floor space to do a few jumping jacks without knocking over a lamp.
- **Hobby/Craft Zone:** A space where your creative pursuits live, with supplies organized and accessible so you actually use them instead of just collecting them.
- **Laundry Zone:** This includes spaces for sorting, folding, and putting away clothes. Because we all know laundry is a journey, not a destination.
- **Utility Zone:** A place for household tools, maintenance items, and possibly cleaning supplies, that's organized enough for you to find what you need when something breaks.
- **Reading Nook:** A cozy corner specifically for getting lost in books, which can be separate from your general relaxation zone if reading is an important part of your life.
- **Meditation/Wellness Zone:** A quiet space for practices that support your mental health, whether that's meditation or journaling.
- **Entertainment Zone:** Where you engage with media like TV, music, or gaming. Or more analogue entertainment like board games, billiards, or babyfoot.
- **Children's Play Zone:** A designated area where kids can be kids, and their toys can live, without taking over your entire existence.
- **Outdoor Zones:** Don't forget about outside spaces! These might include gardening zones, outdoor dining areas, or relaxation spots.
- **Getting Ready for the Outside World Zone**: A space that makes your morning routine more streamlined, with everything you need to get out the door without the daily "where are my keys/wallet/bag/hat/shoes/gloves/coat/lipstick/sanity" panic.

> Well, that's great if you have a 14-bedroom estate, Estelle, but I live in what's essentially a fancy closet.

> That's totally fine. Zones don't have to be entire rooms.

A zone can be:

- A corner of a room
- A specific piece of furniture (like a desk or crafting table)
- A shelf on a bookcase
- A drawer in your kitchen
- Even a box, basket, or bin that holds specific supplies

If you live in a studio apartment or only have a bedroom to call your own, you can still create zones within that limited space. Your bed is the sleep zone, a corner with a desk becomes the work zone, and a comfortable chair by the window becomes the relaxing zone.

The physical boundary is less important than the mental one: each zone has a specific purpose, and your brain learns to associate that space with that activity.

Prioritizing Your Zones

Now, unless you indeed have a 14-bedroom mansion (I'm waiting for the invite), you probably can't (and shouldn't) create all these zones. At least, not all at once.

> Ready for decision time?

> As ready as I'll ever be, Estelle!

Great, let me introduce you to your impact-first matrix. Actually, you've already worked with this concept last week when you picked a task, but let's formalize it. This week, we're going to find which zone could have the most significant positive impact on your life right now with the minimum effort. It's scheduled for day 5, but if you're inspired to do it now, don't stop yourself.

Start by dumping all the zones you need, have, or would like. I would recommend using Post-it notes. Then arrange them on the matrix, thinking:

1. How much impact would it have on my life if this zone were in a functional state?
2. How much effort would I need to create or make this zone functional?

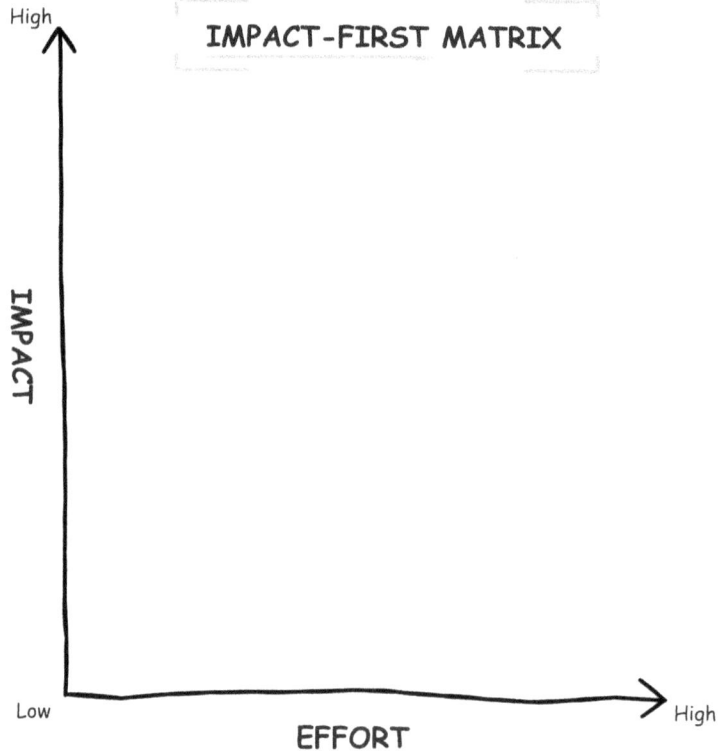

Then, based on your answers, put your zones in the following categories:

1. **Primary Zones:** These are your high-priority spaces and need immediate attention as they will significantly impact your daily life. They're likely to be spaces you use the most: work zone, cooking zone, sleep zone, etc.

2. **Secondary Zones:** You'll tackle once your primary zones are functioning well. Either because the impact will be smaller, or because the task of getting them functional is too overwhelming to start with them.
3. **Unnecessary zones**: Feel free to scrap entire zones in the high-effort + low-impact corner.

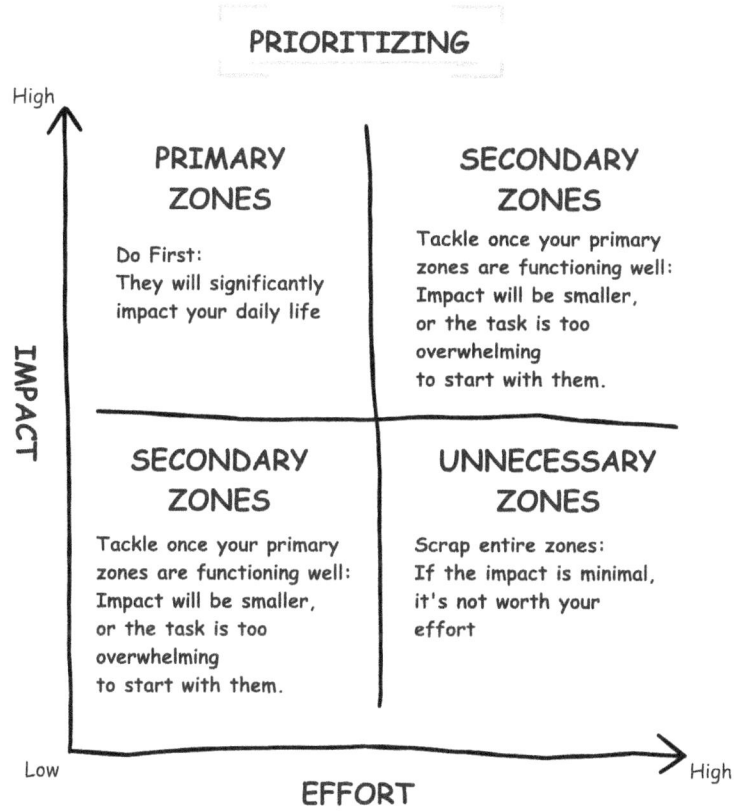

WHEN ZONES OVERLAP

So, what do we do when zones overlap? Either because you're living in a tiny space and even primary zones need to share, or because you'd like to have a zone for a special interest but can't give it a whole room.

Either way, that's completely fine! The key is being intentional (yes, again) about how zones share space. Here are three ways you can create those imaginary boundaries:

1. **Time-based sharing**: The dining table becomes a work zone during the day and a dining zone in the evening.
2. **Visual boundaries**: Use furniture arrangement, rugs, screens, or even lighting to create psychological boundaries between zones that share physical space. If your sofa is turned away from the desk, you can't see your work zone while you're in the relaxing zone. If your desk faces the window, you can't see your entertainment zone while working.
3. **Transition signals**: Create small rituals or changes that signal to your brain when a space is shifting functions. Maybe when the laptop closes and a placemat goes down, the work zone officially becomes the dining zone.

The beauty of zones is that they're entirely customizable to your space, needs, and lifestyle. There's no right way to do this. There's just the way that works for you and your ADHD brain.

3. BEYOND FUNCTIONING

So now that we know *how* to declutter and that we've picked your zones, it's time to zone in further and think about how they're going to support us and our brains. Let me introduce you to environment design.

As a little note, if you're following the 28-day framework, you might not implement any of this until Week 4. That's fine. For now, we're just getting familiar with these concepts as you declutter and design your zones. Consider it advanced scouting for Future You.

Environment is one of the two major levers we have in habit formation and behavior change. The other one is ourselves, which we tackled in Week 1, when we worked on our relationship with organization.

In many ways, tweaking your environment is the easier option. Things don't talk back or have emotional breakdowns when you try to change them. Unlike, you know... us. My coffee table has never once said, "But I've always been cluttered! This is just who I am!" while dramatically slamming a door.

Making Good Habits Easier (and Bad Habits Harder)

When designing a zone, think about what behaviors you want to encourage or discourage in that space, then set it up accordingly.

For instance, in your sleep zone, if you're a chronic snooze-button-hitter (I see you, "just five more minutes" people, you're most of my clients), try placing your alarm clock across the room. That way, you physically have to get out of bed to turn it off. By the time you've done that, you're already up! Your sleepy brain can't outsmart your environment design.

On the flip side, try to make good habits easier. For instance, if you want to exercise more regularly, create a space where your exercise equipment is already set up and ready to go. When the barrier to entry is literally just "step onto the mat," you're much more likely to actually do it than if you have to dig through a closet, set up equipment, and change clothes before you even start.

You're creating a world where your default options are the better choices. It's like having a responsible adult making decisions for you, except that adult is you, just a cleverer version who planned ahead.

Flow and Transitions: The Choreography of Your Home

Another key element is thinking about flow: how you naturally move within and between zones. Consider the sequence of actions you typically take.

For years, my morning routine involved a chaotic back-and-forth between rooms. After taking a shower, I'd head to the bedroom to get dressed, then I'd realize all my skincare products were in the shower room, so I would head back to start applying moisturizer on my face, and go back to the bedroom to get dressed. But I'd then remember I had not put deodorant on, so back to the shower room. I would eventually get dressed, go downstairs, pour myself a coffee, then go back up just before heading out to finish with sunscreen (yes, even in cloudy England) and lipstick.

It was like playing a particularly inefficient game of personal care pinball. And it was all stemming from one root cause: I had read somewhere that skincare and makeup live in the bathroom cupboard.

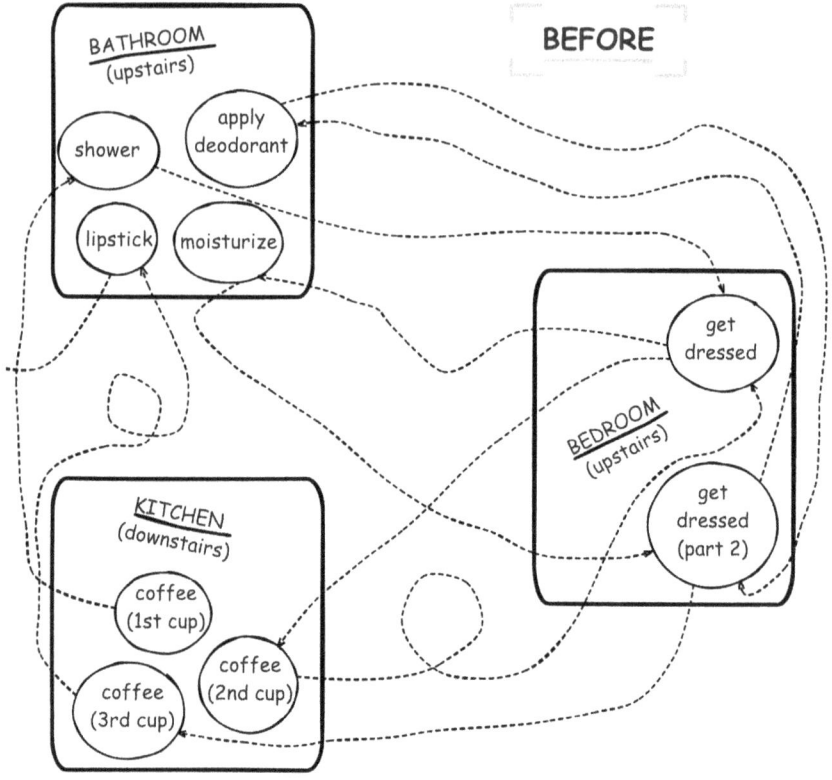

The solution wasn't complicated, but it was transformative: I redistributed my products based on where I actually use them. Morning skincare now lives in my bedroom where I get ready, and just the finishing touches, sunscreen, and that bright lipstick that makes me feel put together even on my most scattered days, stay in the downstairs bathroom for last-minute application after drinking coffee. Now my morning flow makes sense, and I get extra time to literally (and mindfully) wake up and smell the coffee.

THE SENSORY APPROACH

For those of us with ADHD, there's another crucial layer to consider: the sensory environment. It's about how our uniquely wired brains process sensory information.

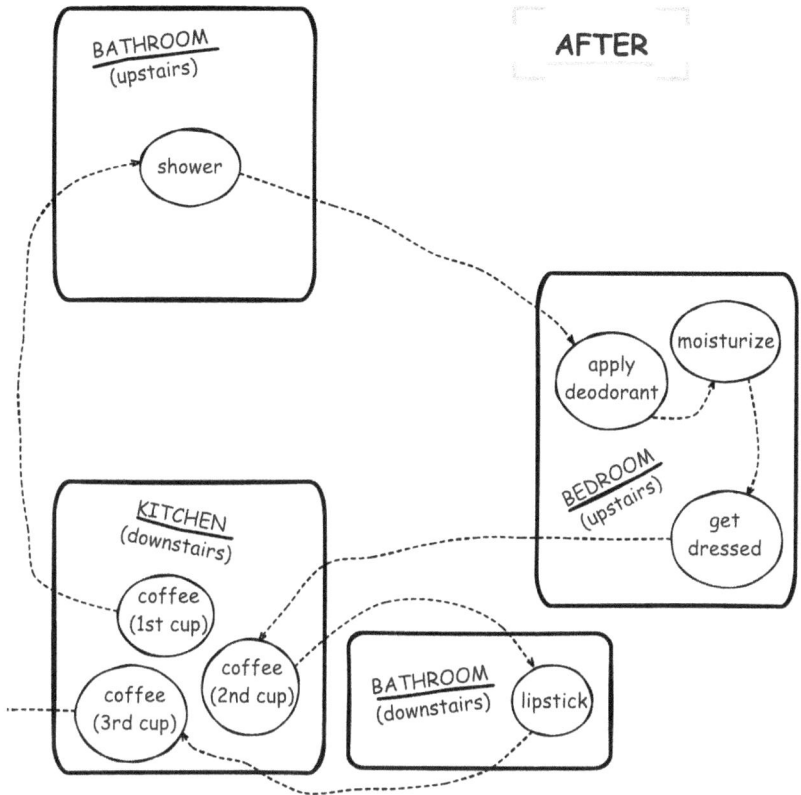

Did you know that 69% of adults with ADHD, studied in a 2019 Dutch study published in *Frontiers in Neurology,* reported an oversensitivity to light? That means more than two-thirds of us might find standard lighting somewhere between distracting and migraine-inducing.

On the flip side, a 2017 pilot study published in the *Journal of Psychiatric Research* found "Bright Light Therapy [...] may be a successful complementary treatment for delayed sleep timing and symptoms of ADHD in adults." Are you one of us? Dreading darker winter months when seasonal affective disorder (SAD) comes knocking on our door with all the subtlety of a wrecking ball?

In Week 4, we'll dig deeper into specific rooms. We'll look at ergonomic modifications, sensory solutions, and other tweaks that can dramatically improve how you function in a zone. But while you might start ~~daydreaming about~~ designing your spaces, consider all five senses:

Sight:

- How are you reacting to light?
- Do you need a neutral palette that calms your visual processing?
- Would an energizing color boost your mood in your exercise or working area?
- Are the items on your walls inspiring, or are they visual noise getting in the way?

Sound:

- Does background noise help you focus, or do you need silence?
- Would a white noise machine help in your sleep zone or work zone?
- Could wind chimes or a small fountain add peaceful ambiance to your relaxation area? Or would that be distracting?

Smell:

- Are there scents that help you focus or relax?
- Could essential oils or candles in specific areas trigger helpful state changes? Maybe that's one of the rituals you need?
- Does your workspace need to be fragrance-free to prevent distraction?

Touch:

- Do certain textures help you feel grounded or comfortable? Could a soft blanket be the trick to turn a socializing zone into a relaxing zone?
- Could different chair cushions make your work zone more functional?

Taste:

- Obviously less applicable to environment design (unless you're planning to lick your walls, which I don't recommend), but can you create zones that make cooking brain-boosting food easier?

- Could a tea station in your wellness zone encourage a calming ritual?
- Would keeping a water bottle on your desk encourage you to stay hydrated while hyperfocusing? Or a flask, minimize distracting trips to the coffee machine?

What calms one ADHD brain might overstimulate another. There's no one-size-fits-all solution, which is excellent news: it means you can create spaces perfectly calibrated for *your* unique brain wiring.

FINAL THOUGHTS

This chapter wasn't just about zones and functions. It was about empowerment. About reclaiming your space from the shame spiral and turning it into something that supports the life you're building, rather than tripping you up every time you try to find your keys or open a cupboard without unleashing an avalanche.

You've learned that zoning isn't about architectural blueprints or needing twelve rooms and a walk-in pantry. It's about creating intention. About drawing invisible lines in the sand and saying, "This space is for rest. This drawer is for admin. This basket is my mental health in fabric form."

Whether you live in a sprawling house or a teeny-tiny studio, you now have the tools to shape your environment to fit you, not the other way around.

The goal isn't just to declutter, zone, label, or bin (although we love a good basket). The goal is to make your space feel like an ally. A quiet little whisper that says, "You've got this. Let's start the day." And reminding yourself (again and again if needed) that it's not about perfection, it's about support.

KEY TAKEAWAYS

- **Functionality and intentionality are key**: Every item we keep should earn its space by being useful now and helping us in our endeavour to make our lives easier. Intentionality turns decluttering from a chore into a conscious act of self-care. When we get clear on why we're doing this and what we need from our space, we start making decisions that genuinely support our day-to-day life (and our ADHD brains).

- **Zoning is a game-changer**: think of it as assigning every activity a home. From sleep zones and work zones to "get out the door without losing your mind" zone, consider all the options, then use the impact-first matrix to focus your energy where it counts. Think: Which zone will have the most significant impact with the least effort? That's where we start.
- **Zones can overlap**: You don't need a spare room for each activity. Shared zones can work beautifully when you're intentional: use time-based sharing, visual cues, or small rituals to switch gears.
- **Environment design can help the Better You**: The layout of your space can either help you build better habits or completely sabotage you. Make good habits easier and bad habits harder. Want to drink more water? Put the bottle where you'll actually see it. Want to snooze less? Move the alarm further. Design for flow and make your routines make sense by thinking about how you move through your space.
- **Your sensory environment matters**: ADHD brains are sensitive. Lighting, texture, sound, and even scent can help or hinder your ability to focus and relax.

week 2 tasks: declutter and design

DAY 1

- Revisit your list of places where things are overflowing (the forensic inspection you took last week on day 5). Is one of those close to where your HITs are? If you've been focusing on washing the dishes, are there too many wooden spoons left on the drying rack? Spices you never use on the countertops?
- Create a donation bag or box. This is going to be your decluttering headquarters for the next three weeks.
- Find ONE thing to get rid of just before or after your HITs, preferably in the same area. Throw it away or put it in the donation box.
- Do your 2 HITs (the old one and the new one you've planned yesterday). They should take under 10 minutes in total.

DAY 2

- Do your 2 HITs
- Find TWO things to get rid of: throw them away or put them in the charity box.
- Consider what you need from your space:
  - Are you working from home and need the ultimate home office, or do you need to collapse in a heap when you're back from work?
  - Do you have certain hobbies? (And I'm not talking about the guitar you bought seven years ago that's gathering dust, I mean hobbies you actually do)
  - Do you have kids whose toys have annexed your living room? Could you all benefit from a play area?
  - Do you like to socialize and entertain at home?
  - Do you exercise at home? Is your treadmill currently functioning as the world's most expensive clothes hanger?

DAY 3

- Do your 2 HITs

- Find THREE things to get rid of
- Choose three words to describe how you want to feel in your home overall. Some examples:
    - Calm
    - Creative
    - Focused
    - Cozy
    - Safe
    - Playful
    - Energized
    - Relaxed

DAY 4

- Do your 2 HITs
- Find FOUR things to get rid of
- Looking back at your reflections from Day 2 this week, start thinking about your zones:
    1. Which activities do I do most frequently?
    2. Where am I experiencing the most friction or stress? Is getting ready in the morning a daily nightmare?
    3. What's causing the most conflict with others in my home? Is family dinner a battleground?
    4. Which change would give me the most significant mental relief?
    5. What aligns with my current capacity and resources? Be realistic about what you can tackle right now. A small, achievable zone creation is better than an ambitious plan that never happens.

DAY 5

- Do your 2 HITs
- Find FIVE things to get rid of
- Based on yesterday's answers, jot down all the zones you'd like in your home, then put them through the impact-first matrix. Which one would have the most significant impact on your well-being? A calming bedroom? A productive home office? Pick your Top Priority Zone, the one with maximum impact and minimum effort, and start targeting it in your decluttering.

DAY 6

- Do your 2 HITs
- Find SIX things to get rid of from your Top Priority Zone
- How are your two HITs going? Consider adding a third one, either in the same room/area as the previous two or, if it's not in your Top Priority Zone, start a third HIT there.
- Think about your Top Priority Zone and collect information:
    - How do I want to feel in this zone? Pick one word.
    - What behaviors do I want to encourage here?
    - What behaviors do I want to make more difficult?
    - How can I arrange my environment to support my goals rather than sabotage them?

DAY 7

- Do your 2 or 3 HITs
- Find SEVEN things to get rid of from your Top Priority Zone
- Take your donation items to the charity shop, empty the bins, or go to the dump. If you plan on selling things, list them now or put them in your donation box. Be honest: if you haven't listed those "valuable" items by now, you might never get round to it.
- Start reflecting on your senses. You can simply be more mindful and notice how you react to certain stimuli, or if it's helpful, start a sensory journal, jotting down any links you find between sensory inputs and your behaviors. You can also start experimenting with different lighting, sounds, or textures in your spaces. Future You will thank you when we put it into practice in Week 4.

week 3: building momentum

CHAPTER FIVE
the art of following through
HOW TO MAKE MAINTENANCE EFFORTLESS

FIRST, take a deep breath and pat yourself on the back. You've made it to Week 3! You've started clearing spaces, you've identified your zones, and you're beginning to see some progress. That's huge.

> But I've been here before, Estelle.
>
> I've had those bursts of organizing energy. I've experienced that fleeting moment of 'I've finally got my life together!' only to watch it all slowly slip out of my hands.

> I get it.
>
> But we're hopping off that hamster wheel now.

You know the cycle we're talking about. It usually starts with an organizing binge, then it's followed by a period where we're enjoying the order and promise we'll keep it that way, but we're exhausted by the frenzy we've just been through. So we let things slide, the clutter creep starts, and soon enough it becomes a clutter overload. It's so overwhelming it triggers task paralysis until we finally hit rock bottom or some external motivation drops from the skies (like moving house), which prompts us to start another organizing binge.

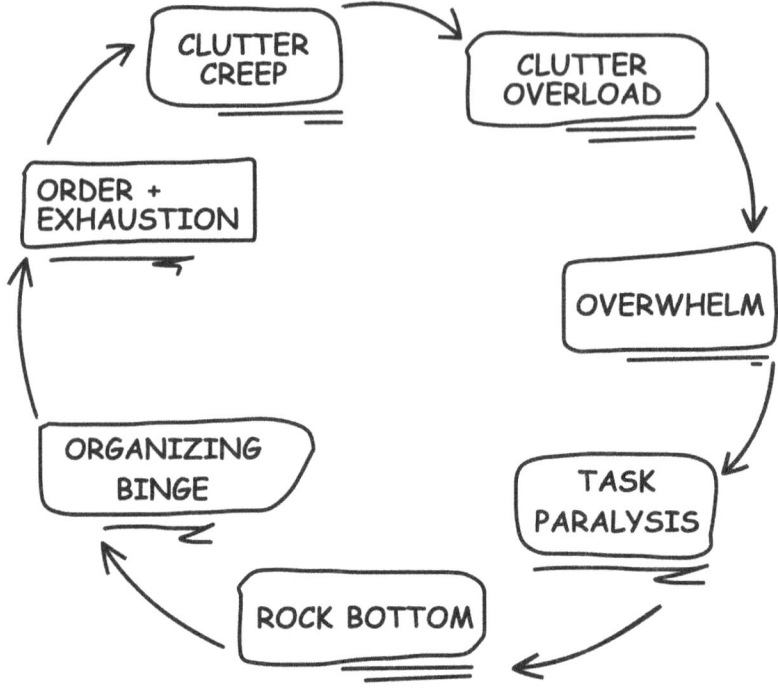

There is another way. What if, instead of relying on motivation (about as reliable as the weather in England), we could build systems that worked even when we don't feel like it?

1. ROUTINES AND RESETS

A huge part of this system is building the right routines and resets. And they're not here to judge you. They're here to help. Like that friend who quietly reminds you to grab your keys before leaving the house, saving you from a lockout.

Less Willpower, More Autopilot

Here's the best part about routines: they're the opposite of discipline.

I know, counterintuitive, right? But think about it: do you need iron willpower to put on a seatbelt when you step into your car? Probably not. You just do it automatically: click, done.

That's the beauty of habits. With enough consistency, actions become predictable. And predictable actions require way less effort from our executive function than constantly deciding, "should I do this now or later? Should I start with this or that?"

So our new cycle will look something like this: You establish a simple routine. With repetition, it becomes more automatic, which requires less mental load. Because it doesn't feel as challenging, we don't procrastinate and get things done, which triggers that little spike in dopamine (that rewarding feeling) which, in turn, reinforces the routine.

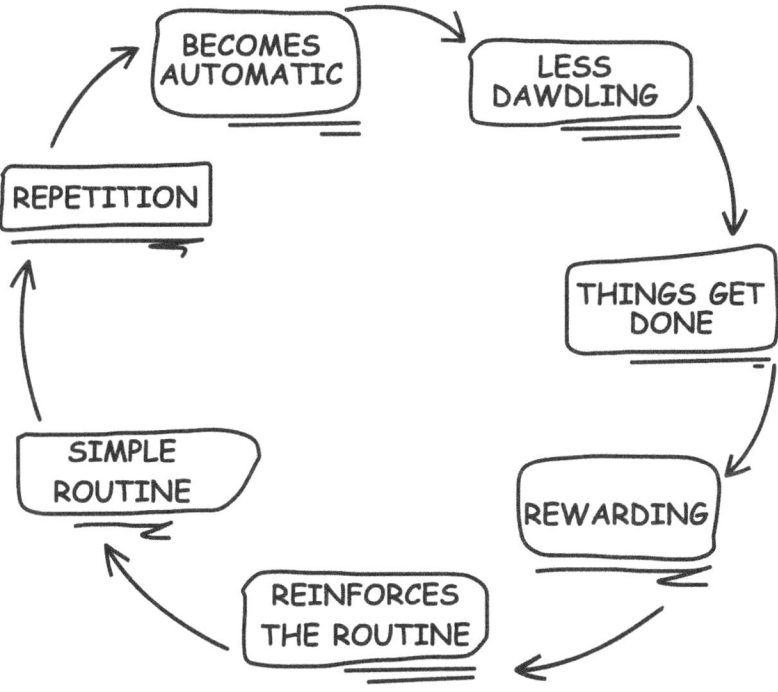

And just like that, you've created an upward spiral instead of a downward one. Did my organizational-loving heart just skip a beat? Maybe.

Your Organizational Scaffolding

Let's talk about resets. Some people call them protocols or rituals, so feel free to come up with your own fancy name. "The Royal Returning Ceremony" has a nice ring to it.

Whatever the name, a reset is simply returning your space to a functional baseline state. Notice I didn't say "perfect" or "the best it's ever been." I said functional, as in serving your needs and making your life easier.

Daily Resets: Small Actions, Big Impact

Remember those High-Impact Tasks (HITs) you've worked on throughout Week 1 and 2? Congratulations, you've already started building your daily reset! These small, daily actions keep the wheels from falling off your organizational cart.

Your daily resets should answer the question: "What needs to happen for me to function well in this space today/tomorrow?" For me (and my family), that includes:

Morning Reset:

- Empty the dishwasher so dirty dishes have somewhere to go during the day, which keeps the surface tops clear so I can cook brain-boosting food.
- Put yesterday's outfit back in the wardrobe or laundry basket to avoid the dreaded "chairdrobe" effect that gets in the way of relaxing.
- Make the bed (in under 3 seconds), transforming my bedroom into my relaxing zone.

Evening Reset:

- Load and run the dishwasher so I don't wake up to yesterday's mess.
- Quick wipe over the kitchen table and countertops.
- Quick kitchen floor swipe.
- Pack leftovers for the next day's lunch, ensuring my brain gets the fuel it needs.
- Quick living room reset (mostly throwing kids' stuff into a basket) to switch from play zone to socializing/entertainment zone.

Your daily resets are about micro-tasks. They shouldn't take more than 10-15 minutes total, even if you have a big household and are the one doing it all. That's the whole point! We're aiming for small, consistent actions that maintain order rather than massive cleaning sessions that burn you out.

Weekly Resets: The Deeper Maintenance

Weekly resets handle the stuff that would be overkill to do every day, but can quickly lead to clutter overload if left too long.

You want to give them a designated day and schedule it to make sure they happen. You can bunch these together into a single "reset day," or distribute them throughout the week in smaller bites if that works better for you.

There's no correct answer here. It depends entirely on your schedule, your energy patterns, who else lives with you, and whether they are taking part.

These might include:

- Meal Planning and Prepping Day, if healthy eating is a priority
- Shopping Day: restocking essentials before you're eating condiment sandwiches
- Laundry Day(s): and yes, I mean the whole process from throwing it into the wash to putting it back in the wardrobe
- Kitchen Day: to give it a proper clean beyond the quick daily reset
- Bathroom Day: because, well... you know why

If they look overwhelming as a list, don't worry. I can guarantee you that it will save you time. And just like your daily reset, we'll build up to it, starting with the minimum effort and maximum impact.

> Don't tell anyone, but I don't clean the oven or under the microwave every single week.

> Okay, gotcha. It doesn't need to be perfect.

> Your secret is safe with me, Estelle.

> Appreciated, neurospicy friend.

Seasonal Resets: The Quarterly Refresh

Then, we have seasonal resets. That's for those bigger-picture tasks that keep your systems running smoothly over time. They could be:

- **Special holiday decor** - Down with the skeletons, up with the bobbles.
- **Wardrobe rotation** - Swapping winter sweaters and coats for summer tanks and swimming costumes. There's something delightful about rediscovering clothes you haven't seen for months. Plus, it creates a natural opportunity to re-evaluate what deserves to stay in your closet. If I haven't chewed your ear about capsule wardrobe in a previous book, don't worry, it's coming.
- **Decluttering sessions** - If you don't feel on top of regular decluttering within your daily or weekly reset, scheduling them regularly can be very helpful to prevent gradual clutter creep.
- **Maintenance tasks** - It's anything that doesn't need to happen weekly but would still be nice to do regularly. Think window cleaning, dusting, carpet cleaning, etc. Or cleaning your patio, ready to enjoy the return of the sun. And if you're wondering about things like dusting ceiling fans… honestly, you're already winning at life.

The beauty of all these resets is that they create a rhythm to your organizational life. Rather than waiting until things reach crisis level, you're making small, consistent deposits into your organizational bank account. You'll build them through this 28-day journey and keep tweaking them way beyond.

2. GETTING DOWN TO IT

So we've got resets, but we both know there's a gap between "I should do this" and actually, you know, doing it.

Allow me to paint you a familiar picture: It's 8 PM. You've just finished dinner. The dishes are scattered across your kitchen counter, stove, and dining table. Your daily reset routine clearly states "load dishwasher after dinner," but somehow you find yourself doom-scrolling on the couch, telling yourself "I'll do it in five minutes" for the eighth time.

The thing is, those of us with ADHD don't just struggle with staying on task, we struggle with *starting* tasks.

Getting started

Although we call it procrastination, transitioning from one task to the next is often what's tricky. It's not that we don't want to do the thing (okay, sometimes we really don't want to do the thing), but more often than not, our neurology makes the shift from one state to another exceptionally difficult.

Transitioning

Have you heard of the 5-second rule? No, not the one about eating food off the floor. This is Mel Robbins's technique: when you need to do something, count backward from 5, and then physically move toward the task and start doing it.

5... 4... 3... 2... 1... MOVE.

This works because it short-circuits your brain's overthinking process. By the time your brain starts listing all the reasons you should stay put, you're already running water in the kitchen sink. I'll be honest, though: this isn't always an ADHD friendly technique in my opinion.

> Why? It sounds so simple!

>> Yes, but often, we forget to even use the 5-second rule.

But I find that becoming aware of transition difficulties helps recognize when we're in transition resistance: "Oh, I'm just struggling with transitioning, that's all it is." And that awareness alone is often enough to break the spell and propel us from chair to dishwasher.

Just start

One of my favorite tricks is the "just start" approach. That's it. Just start putting one shirt back. Just run the tap in the sink. Just put one plate into the dishwasher.

Because here's the magic: starting is almost always the most challenging part. Once you've put that one shirt back into the wardrobe, the momentum often carries you through a few more items. Before you know it, you're halfway through the pile.

The key is making that first step ridiculously small. So small that your brain can't even bother to resist it. "Seriously? You can't grab ONE sock? Come on, that's just sad."

An alternative I also like is The One-Minute Rule, where we tell ourselves, "I'm just going to do this for one minute." Then, if we feel like carrying on, we do; if not, we're allowed to stop.

But these are 'tricks' when resistance is high, and that can be very helpful. But you know what I think of 'tricks'? They're not always sustainable as they're not working *with* our brains.

So here are sustainable techniques that do.

Make It Effortless (Or Less Effort-Full)

Remember how we talked about environment design in Chapter 4? The same principle applies to tasks. We want to make our desired actions as friction-free as possible to make tasks so easy, they require minimal willpower in the first place.

Habit Stacking

This is where habit stacking comes in handy. And I don't mean vaguely deciding to "clean after dinner." I mean getting extremely specific and attaching a new habit to an existing habit. Something so automatic, you don't even think about it.

For instance, I wanted to establish the habit of emptying the dishwasher every morning. I could have set seventeen reminders and eventually ignored all of them. Instead, I linked it to something I did without fail every single morning: making my first cup of tea.

Now, as the kettle boils, I empty the dishwasher. The beautiful part? Boiling the kettle and letting the tea brew takes about the same amount of time as it takes me to empty the dishwasher, so I get a built-in timer. By the time I'm sitting in front of my mug, the kitchen is ready for a new day.

The trick with habit stacking is to:

1. **Identify a genuinely automatic habit**, something you truly do without thinking. Think *really* tiny here. Ridiculously tiny:
   - Putting your feet on the floor when you get out of bed
   - Closing the front door when you come home

- Tying your shoes before going out
- Turning the lights off before bed
- Waiting for your computer to boot up, etc.

2. **Make sure the new habit is in the same location and ideally follows the same rhythm.** In my example, both boiling the kettle and emptying the dishwasher are in the kitchen and are a daily occurrence.
3. **Keep the new habit small enough to feel doable.** Note how I wasn't planning on cleaning the whole kitchen while the kettle is boiling.

Task Bundling

If habit stacking is about sequence, task bundling is about simultaneity: pairing something you don't love with something you genuinely enjoy.

For years, I viewed folding laundry as a special form of torture. Then I discovered audiobooks. I'm almost disappointed now when I run out of clothes to fold because it means pausing the content.

This works beautifully for routine tasks that don't require much mental bandwidth: cleaning, folding clothes, vacuuming, etc. I don't recommend it for decluttering, which demands actual decision-making and can't be done on autopilot.

A good place to start is to ask yourself: What would make this tedious task properly fun? Maybe it's:

- Blasting music and having a mini dance party while you're decluttering
- Calling a friend as you clean the bathroom
- Singing out loud while washing dishes
- Watching a guilty-pleasure show while meal prepping

You're the only one with the answer, but the more enjoyable you can make it, the more it will stick.

If you want to drill down more into habit formation, you could dive deeper into these techniques by reading *Atomic Habits* by James Clear.

FINAL THOUGHTS

This chapter is the glue. The thing that turns all that effort into actual, lasting change. This isn't about becoming some hyper-productive robot who never leaves a dish in the sink. (Spoiler: I left one this morning. It's fine.) It's about switching from binge-clean → burnout → avoidance → shame… to a gentle, steady rhythm you can sustain.

We're not chasing perfection. We're building a scaffolding of daily resets that support your brains, weekly rhythms that keep the chaos in check, and seasonal touchpoints that let you breathe and take stock.

And when motivation ghosts you? You've got tools now. You know how to recognize transition resistance instead of blaming yourself. You've got habit stacking and task bundling in your back pocket. You've learned how to trick your brain with compassion, not punishment. That's you, shifting from fight-or-flight to flow.

Because following through isn't about trying harder, it's about making it easier to show up. It's about celebrating the sock you put in the laundry basket instead of shaming yourself for the pile you didn't finish. It's about designing a life that works with your ADHD, not against it.

So here's your permission slip: Keep it small. Keep it doable. Make it yours.

KEY TAKEAWAY

- **Motivation is flaky, systems are faithful:** Build simple routines and resets that keep your space functional even on the days your executive function has left the band.
- **Tiny routines = massive impact**: Daily, weekly, and seasonal resets aren't about perfection: they're about creating a reliable rhythm to maintain order with less effort. Your daily resets should take 10–15 minutes, max. Weekly resets are designated days for maintenance tasks like laundry, food prep, and cleaning bathrooms. It's adulting, but ADHD-friendly.
- **Make it laughably easy to start**: Starting is the hard part, so try the "just start" trick: do the tiniest possible step (put away one spoon, fold one shirt). Momentum builds from there.
- **Mind your transitions:** ADHD brains struggle with switching

gears. Simply recognizing "I'm in transition resistance" can break the spell and help you move forward.
- **Make it effortless:** Stack new habits over old ones you already do on autopilot. Task bundling turns boring into bearable: Pair low-effort tasks with high-enjoyment activities: fold laundry while listening to a podcast, dance while decluttering.

CHAPTER SIX

tidying up with others

(AND YES, CHILDREN TOO)

> Hey, neurospicy friend, here's something you probably don't tell yourself often enough...
>
> You don't have to do this alone. xo

> Thanks, Estelle, that's nice to hear

WHETHER YOU LIVE with others or not, cleaning and organizing can be social activities. Not just because we are social creatures, but because it makes things much easier. So, whether you live solo, with roommates, a bunch of kids, or a pack of labradors, we'll look at how to make the most out of organizing and cleaning with others.

1. GETTING HELP IS NOT CHEATING

Hiring Help

First off, if you have the means to hire help, there is absolutely zero shame in that. None. It's not a moral failing to pay someone to clean your bathroom or your kitchen. It's a recognition of your strengths, limitations, and priorities. It's as much self-care (if not more) than treating yourself to a spa.

That said, getting help doesn't eliminate your need to develop your own systems. A professional cleaner can scrub your shower, but can't create lasting organization systems that work with your unique brain. So while external help is fantastic, you'll still want to be involved in decision-making.

And free help is fine too, if it's on offer! We'll cover how to have those conversations in just a minute.

Body Doubling

One of the most effective ADHD strategies is body doubling: having someone else physically present while you work on a task. Their mere presence helps keep you accountable and on track.

In my home, our "Sunday Morning Resets," when everyone tackles their weekly reset tasks at the same time, came from a need for body-doubling. My need, the children's need, and probably my husband's too (but he'll never admit it).

We'll talk about tidying up with kids in just a sec. But regardless of the age of the people you live with, the social energy keeps everyone motivated, and nothing says "I should probably get up and do something" like watching your partner industriously scrubbing while you're in your pajamas scrolling on your phone.

If you live alone, virtual body doubling is a great option. At the time of writing, the Empowering ADHD Club body-doubling virtual space is available 24/7 for members to log on and work on their tasks simultaneously. There's something powerful about knowing other people are watching you fold your socks. In the least creepy way possible, of course.

2. COMMUNICATION IS KEY

Clear communication about cleaning expectations is crucial, regardless of who you live with.

But let's be honest, conversations about household chores can get tense fast. One minute, you're calmly discussing who should take out the trash, and the next, you're rehashing that time they forgot your birthday in 2017.

Here's how to have that honest conversation without it turning into a four-hour therapy session or passive-aggressive Post-It war:

Step 1: Set the Stage for Success

- **Time it right**: Don't ambush someone as they walk in the door from work or when they're rushing out. Schedule a specific time when everyone is relatively relaxed.
- **Create the right environment**: Maybe it's over coffee at the kitchen table, not while standing in the mess that's frustrating you.
- **Frame it positively**: "I'd love to talk about how we can make our home work better for all of us" feels very different from "We need to talk about how you never clean up after yourself."

Step 2: Start with Your Own Experience

Begin by sharing how clutter and disorganization affect *you* personally: your stress levels, your ability to focus, your mood, etc. Use "I" statements instead of accusatory "you" statements, like "When I wake up to dishes in the sink, I feel overwhelmed and down before my day even starts."

Step 3: Invite Others to Share Their Experience

This is crucial! After you've shared, genuinely ask how others experience the space, regardless of their neurological labels (remember, learnt behaviors matter, too). It could be: "Are there organizational systems that would make your life easier?"

Listen without interruption or defensiveness. You might be surprised to discover your partner has been silently struggling with something completely different from what you expected.

Step 4: Find Common Ground

Look for areas where your needs align. Maybe everyone agrees that the kitchen needs to be functional in the morning, or that the living room should be a relaxing space.

Step 5: Be Specific About What You Need

Vague requests lead to frustration. Instead of "I need more help around the house," try: "I'd really appreciate it if we could establish a 5-minute kitchen reset that we could do all together after dinner."

Step 6: Play to Everyone's Strengths

Everyone might as well do what they're good at, or like the most, or dislike the least. Ask yourself and share your answer with others:

- What cleaning tasks do you actually not mind doing?
- Are there certain times of day when you have more energy for chores?
- Would you rather do a few things daily or tackle more in one weekend session?

The goal is to divide responsibilities in a way that feels fair but also accounts for preferences and strengths.

Step 7: Create a Concrete Plan Together

Based on your discussion, draft a simple plan that includes:

- Who is responsible for what tasks
- When will these tasks happen
- How often do they need to be done
- What "done" actually looks like (this prevents the "but I DID clean it!" debates)

Step 8: Build in Check-Ins and Flexibility

Agree to revisit your plan after a few weeks. What's working? What isn't? Your needs and schedules will change, and your systems should evolve too. Also, as we ADHD creatures crave novelty, you might fancy swapping at some point.

Step 9: Express Appreciation

When others follow through on their commitments, notice and thank them specifically. "I really appreciated coming home to a clean kitchen yesterday" can go a long way. And while you're at it: give yourself a regular (if not daily) pat on the back for doing your resets, too.

Step 10: Emphasize Progress Over Perfection

Throughout this conversation and the following implementation, regularly remind everyone (yourself included!) of *why* you're doing it. Hint: You're creating a functional space that supports everyone's well-being.

Celebrate improvements rather than focusing on what's still not ideal.

"Hey, we've kept the entryway clear for a whole week, high five!" is worth acknowledging, even if other areas are still works in progress.

And if these conversations feel challenging? That's completely normal. We're talking about where deeply personal habits meet shared spaces, it's complicated territory. But with patience, humor, and genuine curiosity about others' experiences, you can create household systems that work for everyone. Even children. Talking of whom...

3. TIDYING UP WITH CHILDREN

Let's start with the uncomfortable truth: your children absorb your relationship with organization like little emotional sponges. If tidying up makes you tense, frustrated, or triggers a stream of negative self-talk, they internalize all of it.

This was the biggest pill for me to swallow. When I noticed my children mirroring my stress around cleaning, I realized they were reflecting exactly what I had unintentionally taught them.

So before we dive into practical strategies, remember that modeling matters most. All the clever systems in the world won't override the fundamental message your children receive when they see your authentic reactions to maintaining your home.

The good news? This works both ways. When you reframe tidying as a reset, as something that helps your brain feel calmer, as a form of self-care rather than drudgery, they'll begin to absorb that perspective too.

Containers Are Your Best Friends

If there's one organizational tool that makes the biggest difference with kids, it's containers: baskets, bins, bags, trays, anything that creates a boundary around their belongings.

The beauty of containers is threefold:

1. They simplify cleanup (just toss everything in)
2. They create clear homes for categories of items
3. They can make transitions between spaces easier

One strategy that works particularly well is having containers that can move with the activity. For instance, if your child wants to play with blocks in the living room, the entire bin comes along. When playtime is over, all blocks go back to the bin, and the bin returns to its home.

Containers are also very helpful for getting ready and out the door. In our home, we have:

- Activity bags that stay packed and ready (swimming bag, karate bag, beach bag, etc.)
- A big box housing all those activity bags
- Drawers with hats and gloves by the coats
- Toys and activity bins that can travel between rooms as needed, and then go back on a shelf

We're All In It Together

Remember our chat about body doubling earlier? That magical phenomenon where another person's presence helps your brain stay on task? Turns out: it works wonders with children.

The classic parent move is to send kids to their bedrooms with the instruction to "clean this mess up!" Instead, try cleaning alongside them. Not necessarily in the same room, maybe it is the perfect opportunity for you to declutter *your* bedroom. When they see you actively participating, several powerful things happen:

1. They feel less alone in the task
2. They have a model to follow
3. You feel less alone in the task
4. The social energy keeps everyone motivated
5. It becomes a shared experience rather than a punishment

That's why if your schedules allow you to have daily and weekly resets together, you will all have an easier time.

No Charts, No Gold Stars, Just Real-Life Rhythms

Now, while we're talking about modeling, let's also talk about reinforcing these habits.

I don't offer money or rewards for chores, and I don't use chore charts either. I come from the school of thought that tidying isn't a transactional job; it's an act of self-care. I want my kids to see it as part of what we do to care for ourselves and our shared space, not something they need to be paid or externally motivated to do.

Same goes for charts: they're an external motivator and, just like my clients using habit tracking, it doesn't stick long-term. Now, if they work for you, I won't stop you.

So, what has worked? Modeling small, consistent resets as part of everyday life. Teaching kids to tidy not because it earns them a sticker, but because it makes their room easier to play in, or because resetting the living room makes movie night feel cozier. It becomes routine. Expected. Effortless(-ish). That's the rhythm I want to pass on.

Start Early, Build Gradually

The earlier you can begin involving children in organization, the better. An extensive 2019 U.S. study concluded that "performing chores in early elementary school was associated with later development of self-competence, prosocial behavior, and self-efficacy." They even had better math scores, regardless of parental income and education!

For toddlers, begin with the simplest possible rule: one toy or activity out at a time. Before a new activity comes out, the previous one goes back. This creates the foundational habit of returning items to their homes.

As they grow, their responsibilities can expand organically. Of course, every child is different, but here is a very loose framework:

- **Ages 0-3** - Create rituals, like playing the same upbeat "reset song," while helping put toys in bins, and make it part of transition times (before dinner, before bedtime). When playing: one toy out = previous toy goes back in.
- **Ages 4-6** - Build on those rituals to get them involved in room resets with guidance
- **Ages 7-9** - Start handling their bedroom reset more independently. Put things back in communal space (e.g., clear their plates, put food containers back into cupboards). Keep building on rituals (e.g., books, homework, and toys go back where they belong before dinner)
- **Ages 9+** - Keep building on the above and start contributing to family daily and weekly resets (e.g., loading and emptying the dishwasher, wiping the dinner table, swiping, etc.)

- **Ages 11+** - All of the above + Take increasing responsibility for personal spaces and belongings (e.g., putting clean laundry back in closets, emptying bins from their bedroom)
- **Ages 13+** - All of the above + Take increasing responsibility for family resets (e.g., vacuuming, folding their laundry)

Is it perfect? Absolutely not. Do I sometimes have to bite my tongue when the table still has crumbs or the floor still has Choco Pops hiding under the chair? You bet. But the progress is real, and watching them develop these skills fills me with a quiet pride I never expected to feel about dishwasher-loading capabilities.

Everyone Needs a Sanctuary

At the risk of sounding controversial, I would advise keeping at least one room in your home as a child-free zone.

I'm not suggesting your children shouldn't be allowed to enter this space. Rather, this space should be free from toys, children's books, and the general kid-related accoutrements that tend to spread throughout the house.

For me, this sanctuary is my bedroom. It's the one place where I can retreat for a moment of peace, where I don't have to step over Legos or move stuffed animals to sit down.

This might not be possible if you have tiny children, and that's completely understandable. But as your children gain independence, carving out this small haven can be remarkably restorative for your mental health.

FINAL THOUGHTS

Whether those humans are tiny tornadoes of glitter and snack crumbs, a partner who loads the dishwasher "wrong", or a roommate who thinks clutter is a form of interior design, this chapter is your reminder that organization is a team sport. This is about creating a space that works for everyone, not just the one who reads the organizing books (hi, friend, you're my favorite). That means practicing clear communication, making time for gentle resets, and, when possible, sharing the load.

And if you live solo? You're still not alone. You can body-double virtually. Ask a friend for moral support. You can build habits with Future You in mind.

The truth is, homes are ecosystems. They thrive when everyone contributes, when everyone's needs are considered, and when the culture inside them reflects care, not criticism. That goes for kids, too. Let's normalize homes that aren't perfect, but peaceful-ish. Not pristine, but functional. Not chore charts and bribery (unless that's genuinely your jam), but daily rhythms that feel good to live in.

Now, I want to be real: some days, your five-minute reset might stretch to fifteen because your child needed help or got distracted. Some weeks, your Sunday reset might be abbreviated because soccer practice ran long. That's okay. And when the house is a mess and the reset didn't happen and someone's crying on the floor (possibly you), take a breath. That, too, is part of the process.

So, let's turn the page and talk about what happens when things don't go to plan (spoiler: it's not the end of the world).

KEY TAKEAWAYS

- **You don't have to do this alone**: Whether you live solo or with a full house, tidying can be a shared effort. Cleaning together is not just practical: it's powerful. Body-doubling, and mutual motivation all help reduce the mental load. Hiring help is not cheating, and if it's within your means, outsource with pride, but only you can build the ADHD-friendly systems that help you function long-term.
- **You can't overcommunicate**: Talk about chores like you're on the same team. Avoid nagging. Instead, explain how clutter affects your mood and brain. Ask how others experience the space. Be curious, not critical. Be specific, play to strengths, and revisit often. Don't assume people know what "helping more" looks like. Define tasks, assign ownership, and adapt over time.
- **Start them young**: Research shows kids who do chores early develop stronger self-efficacy, independence, and even better academic outcomes later. No gold stars needed: tidying isn't transactional; it's self-care. Reward systems can be fun in the short term, but for lasting habits, internal rhythms and

everyday resets work better than any sticker chart. Kids mirror your energy: if you frame tidying up as a way to care for your space and mental health, they'll also start to absorb that mindset.
- **Containers are magic**: Baskets, bins, trays... They keep kid chaos contained, create clear homes for items, and make it easier to shift activities and clean up without drama.
- **Create a sanctuary**: Everyone needs one space that isn't a chaos zone. A child-free, mess-free area gives you a nervous system reset, helps you maintain boundaries, and models that everyone in the house, even you, is entitled to peace.

seen the light? share your bright spot!

Starting to see glimpses of your floor again?

Drop a review on Amazon. It's like leaving a flashlight for the next person who's still stumbling around in the dark.

Your words can truly make someone's journey feel less lonely and overwhelming. Even a quick, one-line review can offer the exact encouragement someone else needs to start believing there's hope for their space (and their sanity!).

Unsure what to write? Here are a few prompts to get you started:

- Have you experienced a small but noticeable change or win?
- What's your favorite strategy or idea you've discovered?
- How is the tone of the book, the humour, the graphics? How relatable is it?

Leaving a review is simple:

- Click this link or scan the QR code: mybook.to/ADHDorganization
- Scroll all the way down to the review section.
- Click on "Write a Customer Review," just under the ratings.

That's it! It takes less time than finding your keys in the morning, and your words might just give someone else the courage and comfort to take their first step toward clarity.

CHAPTER SEVEN

debugging your life
HOW TO BUILD SYSTEMS THAT CAN BEND WITHOUT BREAKING

I KNOW you've bought this book with the best intentions. You're probably still feeling that little spark of motivation right now (yay!). But we both know that at some point, between now and the end of your life, some things will go wrong, and that's completely, totally, absolutely okay.

> But, Estelle, I don't understand
>
> I've ticked all the daily tasks so far, I'm committed to this 28-day journey, how can it not work?

> Oh, it will work overall
>
> but life happens, and no 1.0 version of any kind of system comes out without needing a few bug fixes.

The difference between this attempt and all those reels you've saved on socials and forgot to implement is that we're expecting hiccups, and we're planning for them.

Instead of seeing them as evidence of personal failure, we're going to approach them with curiosity and an experimental mindset. Think of yourself as a scientist in the fascinating laboratory of your own life. The key is shifting from "I failed at this system" to "This experiment yielded interesting results."

When something doesn't work, it's not evidence that you're broken or lazy or disorganized by nature. It's simply information that this particular approach, in this particular way, doesn't mesh with your particular brain. And that information is incredibly valuable because it guides you toward what might actually work.

1. FIVE STEPS TO TROUBLESHOOT HABITS THAT JUST WON'T STICK

So let's say you've followed every suggestion in this book: you've identified the perfect habit to stack on a new High-Impact Task (HIT), tried making it fun, and removed all the friction you could possibly remove. You've even set 33 different alarms with increasingly desperate labels like "SERIOUSLY DO THE DISHES NOW." And yet... the habit isn't sticking.

Here's my radical suggestion: If it's not sticking, it's not the right system. Simple as.

And we're not here to force ourselves into systems that don't work. That's what we've been doing our whole lives, and how's that working out for us?

Instead of blaming yourself, run your struggling habit through these troubleshooting questions:

1. Is this task genuinely important?

Sometimes the reason a habit won't stick isn't because you're doing it wrong, it's because deep down, your brain knows it's not that crucial. Maybe you thought you *should* do it because you've read so many good things about drinking freshly pressed grass first thing in the morning, but you don't really, really, really *want* it. You've tried, it tastes gross, and you haven't seen any improvement.

It's perfectly okay to drop tasks that aren't serving you and focus your energy on the ones that make a genuine difference.

2. Is it too much?

Sometimes, no matter how small you think you've made the task, it is still too much.

So, let's say grass juice is working for you (when you remember having it)? Maybe pressing it yourself and leaving the whole juicer to clean is overambitious. It's at least three tasks (making it, drinking it, cleaning) when the habit you're trying to form is 'drinking the juice.'

In this case, you could start with buying ready-made juice and get into the habit of drinking it every morning. Once that sticks, if grass juice is still a priority, you could explore how and when to make your own.

3. Could it work at a different time?

Timing is everything. A habit that feels impossible in the evening might slide effortlessly into your morning routine, or vice versa.

I had read from productivity and organizing gurus that preparing your clothes for the next day is an absolute must in any evening routine, so you don't overload your brain in the morning with decisions. Makes sense, right?

So I tried and tried. I set up reminders, a Post-it note on my bedside lamp, but night after night, I would just dump my clothes on a chair (or the floor once the chair was full) and forget to do it.

After weeks of frustration, I accepted that it simply wasn't working, and I started troubleshooting. I'm much better at everything in the morning. And I get dressed every morning without fail: could it be the perfect habit to capitalize on?

So, I gave myself permission to dump my clothes on the chair in the evening, on the condition that they would go back into the closet (or laundry basket) when I get dressed in the morning. The result? I've maintained a relaxing chairdrobe-free bedroom for years.

4. Could different tools make it easier?

Sometimes the right tool can transform a dreaded chore into something manageable.

Maybe sweeping is a struggle, but a cordless vacuum feels almost fun. Perhaps handwashing dishes is your nemesis, but a small countertop dishwasher would be a game-changer. Or maybe nice-smelling cleaning products could help you almost look forward to using them.

5. How can I?

"How can I" questions are very good at propelling our creative thinking, precisely what we need for troubleshooting. So ask yourself:

- How can I reduce the effort involved? How can I reduce the number of steps?
- How can I make it more straightforward? Maybe you've overcomplicated the system.
- How can I make it properly fun? Maybe the task you've tried to bundle it with is, in fact, not that fun, or the fun has worn off.

Some amount of troubleshooting is to be expected for any system, and sometimes… Life happens.

2. THREE STEPS TO HOLD ON TIGHT WHEN LIFE IS JUST TOO MUCH

Sometimes it's significant events: a new baby, a death in the family, a global pandemic, a move. Other times it's just… everything. That low-level overwhelm where nothing specific is wrong, but you're hanging on by your fingernails nonetheless.

Either way, there will be times when your beautiful organizational systems start to slip because your functionality is very low. And that's not just okay, it's inevitable. The key isn't to prevent these periods (you can't). It's to have the means to climb back once you're ready.

Step 1: Radical Acceptance

First, acknowledge what's happening without judgment. "I'm going through a tough time right now, and my home organization is reflecting that." Period. No "I should be handling this better" or "Other people manage to keep it together when…" Write yourself a permission slip if it helps.

Step 2: Dial It Down (But Don't Turn It Off)

When life gets overwhelming, you don't need to abandon all your systems on the pretext that they're not perfect anymore. You just need to scale them way back to their absolute essentials.

This is where knowing your "cornerstone habits" becomes crucial. Your cornerstone habits are the small actions that, when completed, tend to unlock or trigger a cascade of other positive behaviors.

For me, it's getting dressed in the morning. This might sound ridiculously basic, but on my hardest days, it's my non-negotiable. Because when I get dressed, I naturally do a series of connected actions: I put yesterday's clothes in the hamper, I make my bed (because I need somewhere to lay out today's outfit), and I take a cold shower (which helps me focus).

Even if I do nothing else all day, getting dressed keeps a thread of my routine intact. A thread I can gradually build back upon when I'm ready.

Your cornerstone habit might be different. Maybe it's loading the dishwasher every night, even if you don't entirely empty it in the morning, or it's not full because you're living on takeout at the moment.

Whatever it is, identify it as you're building your resets, and when motivation is still reasonably high. Then, when life gets tough, you'll know exactly what to focus on: just that one thing.

Step 3: Remember It's Temporary

When we're in the thick of difficult times, it can feel like things will never improve. But they will. And when you're ready to rebuild your routines, you won't be starting from scratch. The neural pathways you've already established, even if they've gotten a bit overgrown, are still there, waiting to be rediscovered.

In the meantime, be incredibly gentle with yourself. A temporarily messy home isn't a character flaw; it just reflects your current circumstances. And circumstances always change.

FINAL THOUGHTS

This concludes our third week together! Can you start by giving yourself a massive pat on the back? We're done with system building! Next week, we're going around the house to apply it to real-life examples.

So as we move forward with the next chapters and tasks, carry this mindset with you: you're not failing, you're researching. And with each experiment, successful or otherwise, you're building a deeper understanding of what truly helps you thrive.

Because ultimately, that's what this is all about. Not a perfect home, but a space that supports your imperfect, beautiful, complex life. Not a perfect system, but routines that make you feel more at ease in your own skin. Not a perfect you, but a you who knows that messiness in homes and lives is simply part of being human.

KEY TAKEAWAYS

- **Failure is data**: When a system doesn't work, it's not a sign you're broken. It's just information. Treat it like an experiment: "That didn't work yet... let's adjust the variables." This whole process is about building a space and a life that works for you.
- **If it's not sticking, the system is the problem** (not you): Instead of spiraling into "why can't I just do this," ask better questions: Is this task genuinely important? Is it too much? Is it at the wrong time? Are my tools working for me or against me? Sometimes we just need to pivot, not push harder. Small shifts can make a huge difference.
- **Ask "How can I?" to unlock creativity**: "How can I make this easier? More fun? Less annoying?" gets your brain into solution mode. Your inner critic doesn't get a seat at that table.
- **When life gets messy, scale it way back**: Hard seasons happen. Your whole routine may not be doable, and that's okay. Identify your cornerstone habit and gently hold onto it until life softens. These are your personal anchor routines that help rebuild momentum when everything else has fallen away.
- **Radical acceptance beats perfectionism**: Drop the guilt. Write yourself a permission slip if needed. You're doing your best. Overwhelm doesn't last forever. Your systems aren't lost, they're just sleeping. You'll wake them (and yourself) back up when you're ready. Be gentle until then.

week 3 tasks: building momentum

DAY 1

- Do your 3 HITs (they should take under 10 minutes in total)
- Find EIGHT things to get rid of from your Top Priority Zone
- If you haven't already, consider moving to another area to declutter. Where would have the most impact next? What are your other Priority Zones?

DAY 2

- Do your 3 HITs
- Find NINE things to declutter
- Plan to talk with the people you live with (if relevant). Think about which tasks you find easier and which ones you struggle with. What would help make the challenging ones more doable?
- If you live solo, consider remote body doubling. Do you want to ask a friend or look into digital memberships?

DAY 3

- Do your 3 HITs
- Find TEN things to declutter
- Have or schedule that conversation about shared responsibilities if you live with other people.
- Reach out to the person you'd like to body double with or look at body-doubling websites like Flown or the Empowering ADHD Club.
- Make a list of what needs to be done daily and weekly to work toward how you want to feel in your space. Remember to emphasize well-being and impact over perfection!

DAY 4

- Do your 3 HITs (this is now going to become your daily reset)
- Plan your daily reset (morning and evening if relevant)

- Plan your weekly reset(s). Be as precise as you can with when and how. Are you going to batch all weekly tasks on one day or spread them across the week? Remember, this is just an experiment: be ready to adjust to find the right rhythm for you.
- Find ELEVEN things to declutter

DAY 5

- Do your daily reset
- Do your scheduled weekly reset if today is the day (e.g., laundry day)
- Find TWELVE things to declutter
- Plan your seasonal reset: What bigger tasks need to happen a few times a year to keep your space functional?

DAY 6

- Do your daily reset
- Do relevant weekly reset tasks (e.g., bathroom day)
- Find THIRTEEN things to declutter
- Consider starting to declutter another area. What is your next Top Priority Zone?
- Identify your cornerstone habit and non-negotiable: What's the one thing that makes everything else easier when you do it consistently?

DAY 7

- Do your daily reset
- Do your relevant weekly reset (e.g., kitchen day)
- Find FOURTEEN things to declutter
- Donate or throw your decluttered stuff
- Do a little celebration dance: you've made it to Week 4! Look at all those boxes you've ticked and acknowledge how far you've come in just three weeks.

week 4: around the house

CHAPTER EIGHT

making your kitchen adhd-friendly

CREATE A SPACE FOR NOURISHMENT AND SANITY

At this point, you might be starting to feel that subtle shift from "everything is overwhelming" to "hey, this might actually be manageable."

Now we're going to get specific. We're heading room by room through the spaces that tend to cause the most ADHD-related struggles.

> But, Estelle, you said we have to create our own system…

> Right on! I'm not here to tell you exactly how to organize your space.

> This isn't an exhaustive home tour.

> We'll focus on what tends to generate the most chaos for ADHD brains, and when functioning well, can significantly reduce your ADHD symptoms.

> Okay, let's dive in!

Let's start with the kitchen. No matter how small it is, without question, it is still a cooking zone. That goes without saying. But before we jump into solutions, take a moment to consider whether your kitchen serves another purpose:

- Is it also a social hub where your family gathers?
- Does it double as your workspace because you're in a small apartment?
- Is it where your kids spread out their homework?
- Do you use it for crafts or other hobbies?

Understanding all its functions will help you design it to serve you better.

1. CREATING A BRAIN-FRIENDLY KITCHEN ENVIRONMENT

Remember everything we've learnt about intentional environment design? Small tweaks here can dramatically reduce the daily friction that often leads to "I'll just order a takeout".

The Visibility Sweet Spot

The ADHD brain's classic dilemma: "If I can't see it, it doesn't exist" versus "If I can see everything, I'm completely overwhelmed."

This tension plays out dramatically in the kitchen. Those 50 spice jars might look beautiful on an Instagram-worthy spice rack, but do they actually help you cook, or do they create sensory overload? Not to mention the headache they are to clean.

Remember our tier system for storing belongings? Let's apply it to your kitchen items:

Tier 1: "In Plain Sight" (Daily Use Items)

Items you use daily should have prime real estate in your line of sight, right on the counter or open shelving. It's entirely up to you, but it could be a coffee machine, food processor, air fryer, etc. You also want to consider any 'good habit' you're trying to promote: a fancy water jug to remember to hydrate, vitamins or medication, fresh fruits in a nice bowl, etc.

Tier 2: "Easy Access" (Regular Use Items)

Items you use several times a week should be in easy-to-access drawers, the front of cabinets, or grouped in clear containers. Think of your go-to spices, cooking utensils, plates, and cutlery. You want to access these with minimal effort: just a quick drawer pull away.

Tier 3: "Secondary Storage" (Occasional Use Items)

Things you use monthly, like special baking tools or entertaining dishes, can go in less accessible cabinets. They shouldn't take up prime real estate, but you still need a logical home, so you can find them.

Tier 4: "Deep Storage" (Rare Use Items)

Seasonal items, specialty ingredients used once or twice a year, or the turkey roaster that only comes out at Thanksgiving can go in deep storage: high shelves, back of pantries, or even separate storage areas. Just remember to make a list of what is in there so you don't end up buying another turkey roaster. Also, this is not permission to hold on to the "just in case" clutter.

Mapping Your Kitchen Workflow

To design a kitchen that truly works with your brain, take some time to observe your natural patterns. Next time you're cooking, just pay attention to:

- **Where do you naturally set things down?** This is valuable information about where items should "live."
- **What do you constantly have to walk across the kitchen to retrieve?** These might need a new home closer to where you use them.
- **Where do you get stuck or frustrated?** These friction points are prime candidates for redesign.
- **What items do you use together?** These should be stored together

You might want to consider creating micro-zones to reduce mental load. Maybe your coffee station deserves its own dedicated counter space with everything you need for your morning brew.

Environment Design for Brain-Friendly Cooking

Based on your observations, here are some ways to design your kitchen to better support your brain. Remember, they're just ideas. You don't have to implement them all.

Reduce Transition Friction:

- Store cutting boards near where you prep food

- Keep cooking utensils right by the stove
- Place dishes close to where you plate food
- Consider a hanging rack for pots and pans so you don't have to dig through cabinets
- Keep a small compost bin on your counter for food scraps
- Place a recycling bin right where you unpack groceries
- Have cleaning supplies easily accessible for quick wipe-downs

Create Visual Reminders:

- Use clear containers for staples so you can see when they're running low
- Keep a whiteboard, a chalkboard, or a paper pinned on your fridge for meal plans and grocery lists that you can add to as you notice things running low.
- Consider an "eat this first" container in your fridge for items about to expire

2. EATING WELL: FUELING YOUR ADHD BRAIN

If managing your ADHD through nutrition is high on your agenda (smart move!), then having a kitchen that supports healthy eating becomes essential. Your daily resets might already include clearing countertops and tables to create functional cooking space. But a truly supportive kitchen needs one more thing: a plan.

Meal planning and prepping

Planning your meals for the week and shopping accordingly can transform your kitchen organization and eating habits while freeing brain space.

Here are five ways you can make meal planning ADHD-friendly:

- **Go digital with your shopping list** - Create a list you can reuse each week. I keep mine on TickTick, an app I bang on about, in about every single one of my books.
- **Consider subscriptions for essentials** - Many supermarkets offer subscription services for basics like toilet paper, coffee, or household supplies. You can also add a weekly delivery of milk, bread, fruits, and veg.

- **Fresh Meal Subscription** - If you like the idea of cooking fresh food but planning is overwhelming, maybe a cooking subscription is what you need. You'll receive the recipe and all the ingredients you need.
- **Fresh is best, but convenience is okay** - Yes, fresh food is better for our ADHD brains (we don't do well with E numbers and sugar, which processed foods are full of). But if buying pre-chopped vegetables is the difference between eating vegetables and not, then by all means, choose convenience.
- **Batch-prep or batch-cook** - Consider batch-prepping or cooking as part of your weekly reset. If that sounds too overwhelming, just cook an extra couple of portions when you prepare a meal and use them as a healthy lunch, a lazy dinner, or freeze and rediscover in a couple of weeks.

The Great Food Purge

Rotting food items or impulse-purchased tins of jackfruit you'll never eat all count as decluttering.

Remember the container's rule. Your cupboard and fridge can only contain so much, and having to move five packs of half-empty crackers that the kids won't eat because "they've gone soft now" just to find the tomato sauce is friction.

So once you've gone through a food decluttering purge, consider reassessing weekly as part of your kitchen reset. Consider tagging it to another habit like getting the groceries in, meal planning, or writing your shopping list.

3. THE DISHES OF DOOM

Dishes are often the stickiest point in kitchen organization, literally and figuratively. They have a way of spreading across every available surface if left unchecked.

One load a day

My absolute best tip?

1. Run your dishwasher daily, regardless of how full it is.

2. Fit the loading (or pressing start if already loaded) and unloading into your daily reset.

That's it. Thank me later.

And yes, if you live alone, you might run it every other day, but having a system is key.

I held back for years for environmental reasons, but my green concerns were unfounded: When I made this decision, we started including items we didn't use to put in the dishwasher, like pans that used to pile up in the sink. Then by running the shortest cycle and including everything, I'm probably saving water and energy (literally and figuratively), while improving my mental health.

Nothing depresses me more than a sink full of dishes, and this simple rule was as close as it gets to a magic wand.

Hand washing

I'm not talking about global pandemics here, just about washing *by* hand. If you don't have a dishwasher, find a system that works with the cards you are dealt. Here is some inspiration for ADHD-friendly techniques to pick and mix:

- Add dirty dishes to a dish rack or drainer for 24 hours to keep the sink accessible. Then wash everything in one batch as part of your daily reset.
- Wash dishes as you go along throughout the day. Then, if anything is left, wash them all up during your daily reset.
- Put everything to soak overnight to let water and soap work for you and reduce elbow grease.
- Wash dishes first thing in the morning when energy is higher.
- Make washing the dishes more enjoyable, either by:
    - Using it as an opportunity to practice mindfulness. Tune into the experience: what does the water temperature on my skin feel like? What does the soap smell like? Etc.
    - Task bundling: sing along to your favourite tune, listen to the news, your favourite radio show, or a podcast. You get the idea.

Simplify

Remember the basic principle of simplifying? It works here too: the fewer dishes you use, the less you will have to wash.

Here are a few ways you can cut down:

- You don't need to be a chef and use different pots and plates for each recipe step. A single crockpot can make a great, nutritious meal.
- A bowl with a plate on top, or the other way around, becomes instant food storage. No need to transfer leftovers to a Tupperware that will also need washing later.
- Keep one glass per person per day. If they're not matching, you'll know which is whose more easily.
- Keep the same mug while on a coffee or tea drip.
- Unless you're handling raw meat or fish, you can use the same cutting board throughout the day, and just wash it once in the evening. The carrots won't judge that you were cutting bread here in the morning.

FINAL THOUGHTS

When your kitchen works, everything else in life feels just a little more doable. Not because you've suddenly turned into a domestic goddess, but because you've reduced the constant friction.

So if your kitchen looks even a bit clearer, or if the idea of cooking doesn't make you want to cry into a takeaway menu anymore, take a moment to acknowledge that. You're changing your relationship with your space. And that's not small.

This isn't about having a spotless kitchen. This is about building a space that makes your life easier, calmer, and more nourishing, mentally and physically. And whether you're a batch-prepper, a one-pan wonder, or someone who eats cereal out of a mug (no shame), you now have a kitchen that's working *with* you, not against you.

KEY TAKEAWAYS

- **Reduce daily friction**: When you set it up to support how your brain works, you'll spend less time searching and more time functioning. Use the 4-tier system: daily-use items in plain sight, regular-use items within easy reach, occasional-use items tucked away but still findable, and rare-use items in deep storage (with a reminder list!) Watch what you naturally do in your kitchen and arrange your space accordingly. Micro-zones can make a big difference.

- **Meal planning reduces decision fatigue:** Use the tools that work for you (apps, subscriptions, pre-filled lists), batch prep if that feels doable, and focus on realistic choices that support your ADHD brain, not perfection.
- **Decluttering food counts:** Expired items, impulse buys, and those five types of mayo create clutter and friction. A regular kitchen purge keeps your cooking zone functional.
- **Dishes are less dreadful with a system:** Run your dishwasher daily, even if it's not full. If you wash by hand, find the method (and timing) that fits your rhythm.
- **Simplify your dish habits:** Use fewer dishes, repurpose containers, and embrace shortcuts like reusing your mug or chopping board. The fewer the dishes, the easier the cleanup.

CHAPTER NINE
bathroom with a cause
LESS GUILT, MORE GLOW

ALRIGHT, let's talk about that room where many of us start and end our day: the bathroom. For most of us with ADHD, this space becomes the unintentional museum of half-used products, impulse purchases, and those "miracle" solutions that somehow never worked their miracles.

1. SETTING YOUR BATHROOM INTENTION

Before diving into organizing bottles and bins, take a moment to identify your intention for the bathroom.

> Duh, Estelle, it's to get clean.

>> I love that you're taking a functional perspective.
>>
>> But bathrooms can serve us in many other ways.

Ask yourself: How do I want to feel in this space?

Is your bathroom where you need to get energized and find clarity in the morning? If so, your environment design choices could include:

- Waterproof sticky notes to capture those brilliant shower thoughts (yes, these actually exist!)
- Motivational quotes or affirmations on the wall

- Inspirational bath mats
- Bright, energizing colors
- Invigorating scents like citrus or mint
- A shower speaker for upbeat morning playlists

Or is your bathroom a relaxation zone where you decompress and find calm? Then consider:

- Adding plants (many varieties can thrive in bathroom humidity, even with limited light)
- Soft, soothing colors
- A speaker for relaxing sounds
- Candles or essential oil diffusers with calming scents like lavender
- Minimal visual clutter to create a spa-like retreat

Maybe your bathroom needs to boost your self-confidence:

- A mirror with good lighting that makes you feel fantastic
- Visual reminders of your achievements or goals
- Space for skincare or grooming rituals that make you feel your best
- Colors that energize you or make you feel powerful

The point is your bathroom is a space where you're vulnerable, where you prepare to face the world or wind down from it. The environment you create there can significantly impact your mood and mindset throughout the day.

And if you're fortunate enough to have multiple bathrooms, they might serve different functions with different intentions. Perhaps your ensuite is your morning energizing zone while the main bathroom is designed for relaxation and unwinding.

Your intention will guide your organizational choices, sensory elements, and how well the space serves you.

2. THE BEAUTY PRODUCTS GRAVEYARD

Let's be honest: the bathroom will likely be another big decluttering win. Why? Because most of us hoard beauty products like we're preparing for a zombie apocalypse, where the only currency will be hair conditioner and serums.

We've all been there. You're standing in the store, holding that fancy new shampoo, you're telling yourself "I'm worth it", and your brain is lighting up with dopamine at the mere possibility of having the beautiful locks you've always dreamed of.

The cycle is painfully predictable:

1. Buy impulsively
2. Use once or twice
3. Doesn't deliver on promises
4. Keep "just in case"
5. Forget we have it
6. Buy something else impulsively

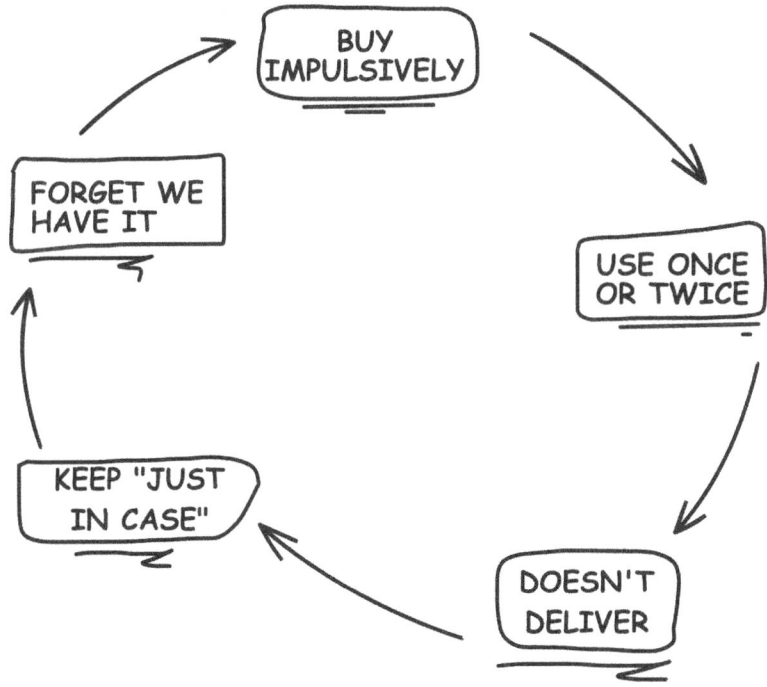

But here's the truth: there is no "just in case." That half-empty bottle of curl gelly you hate the smell of isn't going to become appealing three years from now magically. That face cream that made you break out isn't suddenly going to work on your skin if you keep it long enough.

It's time for an honest conversation with yourself. Most of us use only a handful of products regularly. The rest? They're just taking up space, creating visual clutter, adding to the mental load, and making it harder to clean your bathroom.

So grab a trash bag and take a deep breath. We're going in.

Remember our three decluttering questions from Week 2? Let's apply them specifically to bathroom products:

1. **Do I love it?**
   - Do I genuinely like how this product smells, feels, or works?
   - Does using it make me feel good about myself?
   - If I saw this in a store today, would I buy it again?
2. **Do I need it?**
   - Is this a staple in my routine or just something I experimented with?
   - Is it expired? (Yes, beauty products expire.)
   - Do I already have something else that serves the same purpose but works better?
3. **Do I actually use it?**
   - Has it been sitting untouched for months (or years)?
   - Am I keeping it out of guilt because it was expensive?
   - Am I keeping it "just in case"?

For everything that doesn't pass this test: let it go. If it's in good condition and relatively new, consider passing it along to a friend who might appreciate it. Otherwise, it's one for the bin.

And make yourself a promise: next time you're tempted by that revolutionary curl custard or miracle serum, remember that the best product is the one you'll use consistently. (And yes, I'm not ruling out writing a book about curls, but that's a project for another day.)

3. OPEN VS. CLOSED

The bathroom presents our classic ADHD organizational dilemma: do we keep things out in the open so we remember to use them, or tucked away in cupboards to cut the visual overload and keep the space easier to clean?

Remember my morning routine example and how I've scattered products between bathrooms and the bedroom for a simpler workflow? Things don't necessarily need to be stored where convention says they should be. They need to be where *you* will use them.

If you're trying to decide what stays visible and what gets hidden away, here's a general rule:

Things that can go in closed storage:

- First aid supplies
- Non-daily Medications
- Seasonal products (sunscreen, mosquito repellent)
- Bulk buys (the 5 L bottle of your favorite conditioner that saves plastic and money)
- Genuine "just in case" items (but be very selective here!)

Things that might work better in the open:

- Daily skincare products
- Toothbrush and toothpaste
- Your real-life go-to hair products
- Anything you're actively trying to remember to use

The Tray Trick

For items that need to remain visible and accessible (like shower essentials), trays are absolutely fantastic. Why? Because they:

1. Corral related items together, creating visual order
2. Make cleaning so much easier: just lift the entire tray and wipe underneath
3. Create psychological boundaries that discourage you from adding more stuff

Look for trays that can be lifted in one go when it's time to clean. Extra points if you can find something dishwasher-safe, because let's be real, those trays can get grimy, and being able to toss them in the dishwasher removes yet another barrier to cleaning.

Hanging caddies or shower organizers serve the same purpose for tub/shower items. The key is containment and mobility, making moving things as a unit easier than individually.

4. BREAKING DOWN THE CLEANING BEAST

We typically tackle the bathroom as part of our weekly reset, but that can feel overwhelming for many people. Then it doesn't happen until you start noticing black grease on your bathtub, and the guilt and shame grab you by the throat like a hungry zombie. Not really the kind of feelings we're trying to foster here.

If that's you, consider breaking it down into smaller tasks and adding one a day to your daily reset. Try habit-stacking to things you're already doing in the bathroom:

- Clean the shower while you're in it (keep a squeegee or spray bottle of cleaner in there)
- Hang wet towels properly just as you step out of the shower
- Clean the mirror while brushing your teeth
- Wipe down the sink right after brushing your teeth
- Quickly clean the toilet before bed
- Mop the floor after your bath

I'm not suggesting you need to deep-clean everything daily. I'm saying the prompt for cleaning each small part could be something you already do daily. By the end of the week, you've cleaned the whole room without ever feeling overwhelmed.

I've seen this approach work wonders for people who struggle with finding the time or motivation for a complete cleaning session.

FINAL THOUGHTS

Whether it's a five-minute energizing pit stop, a confidence-boosting prep zone, or your evening wind-down sanctuary, your bathroom can be more than just functional. It can be an intentional space that supports your body *and* your brain.

You need a bathroom that reflects the way you live, where you can find what you need without knocking over three half-empty bottles of conditioner, where you're not cleaning around things you haven't used in five years, where you see a space that feels manageable, supportive, maybe even soothing.

Now that we've scrubbed, sorted, and simplified your bathroom, it's time to shift gears and move into a space that has a direct line to your rest, focus, and overall mental health: your bedroom. Pajamas at the ready, we're heading in.

KEY TAKEAWAY

- **Set an intention for your bathroom**: It's not just where you brush your teeth, it's where you start and end your day. Design it to match how you want to feel in that space: energized, calm, confident, or all of the above.
- **Be honest with yourself:** Keep what you actually use, love, and need, and let go of the guilt clutter. Most of us use only a few staple products regularly. Everything else is just noise (and a cleaning hassle).
- **Storage visibility is a balancing act**: Store your daily essentials in sight but contained, and tuck away the rest. Use trays and containers to create boundaries. They don't just make your bathroom look more put together, they make it easier to clean and less likely to spiral into chaos again.
- **Break down cleaning into micro-tasks:** You don't have to deep-clean the whole bathroom in one go. Tackling a single part of your bathroom daily can feel a whole lot more manageable. Stack cleaning habits onto routines you already do, like wiping the sink after brushing your teeth.

CHAPTER TEN

rest is not a luxury

DESIGN A BEDROOM THAT HELPS YOU SLEEP BETTER AND THINK MORE CLEARLY

THERE WAS a time when my bed was buried under a mountain of clean (but unfolded) laundry. My nightstand had become a precarious tower of half-read books, water glasses, and mugs of tea in various states of emptiness, and at least three different lip balms. The rocking chair in the corner hadn't functioned as actual seating in months. It was now the proud home of clothes that existed in that strange purgatory between "clean enough to wear again" and "definitely needs washing".

Was it conducive to restful sleep? I think you know the answer.

For many ADHD folks, our bedrooms become a catch-all space and the space we target last, because thanks to our people-pleasing tendency, we prioritize social spaces like the kitchen and living rooms.

Yet, sleep isn't just about avoiding under-eye circles, it's about basic brain function.

1. ZONING THE BEDROOM

SLEEP FIRST

One particularly eye-opening study published in *Occupational and Environmental Medicine* found that just one week of sleeping less than six hours per night produced cognitive performance deficits equivalent to having a blood alcohol level above the legal driving limit.

And that's for anyone. For us, many studies, including Stein's 2023, have concluded that ADHD symptoms and sleep problems "are viewed as common and mutually exacerbating conditions." Sounds like another vicious cycle, playing up with our already fragile executive function:

- Working memory? Poor sleep is not going to help that goldfish brain.
- Emotional regulation? Good luck with that on five hours of rest.
- Focus and attention? Sorry, what were you saying?
- Impulsivity? Cranked up to eleven after a bad night.

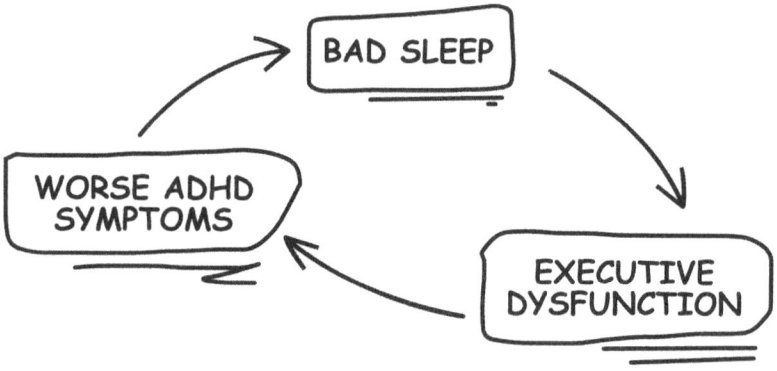

As you know, I try to encourage you to find what works for you throughout this book… but when it comes to bedrooms, I'm going to be a bit more prescriptive: Your bedroom's primary purpose should be sleep because that's one of the most efficient way to improve ADHD symptoms.

If your bedroom must serve multiple purposes, the key is creating clear sensory and visual boundaries between your sleep zone and the other zones.

If you're fortunate enough to have a bedroom that can be solely a sleep zone (and intimate activities if in the mood), embrace this luxury! Go all-in on creating the ultimate sleep environment with sensory design, which we'll cover in the moment.

Now, for everyone else, if your bedroom must serve multiple

functions, don't despair. The key is creating clear sensory and visual boundaries between your sleep zone and other activity zones.

Setting Boundaries

Rule number one: Whatever you do, never ever work from bed. Even if your bed is the most comfortable spot, working from it destroys the psychological association between your bed and sleep. If you must work in your bedroom, establish a dedicated work area that's not your bed.

Here are some practical ways to create those boundaries:

Physical Dividers:

- A folding screen or a curtain can be used as a room divider between your bed and desk
- Furniture arrangement can create natural divisions: a bed facing away from work areas, a strategically placed bookshelf, or even a large plant can create visual separation.
- Furniture you can close: Like a secretary desk that becomes just like a cupboard in the evening, a Murphy or high-rise bed you don't get to see while you work.

Visual Cues:

- Different lighting schemes for different activities (warm, dim lighting for sleep zone; brighter lighting for work)
- Separate color schemes for each zone

Transition Rituals:

- A specific action that signals transition between zones (e.g., closing a laptop and putting it in a drawer, making your bed)
- A designated "closing time" for non-sleep activities. For instance, no work after 8 pm or before 8 am.

Now that we've protected our sleep zone with clear boundaries, let's turn to how to make the magic (and the melatonin) happen.

2. SENSORY DESIGN

Small sensory disturbances can mean the difference between restorative sleep and tossing and turning all night. Let's break down the sensory elements of a sleep-promoting bedroom.

Managing Light

Light might be the most crucial sensory factor affecting sleep quality. Our bodies are programmed to respond to light cues, with darkness triggering melatonin production (the hormone that makes you sleepy).

Here are some essential strategies:

- **Blackout curtains or blinds** - These are non-negotiable for most ADHD brains. Even small amounts of street light or early morning sun can disrupt sleep quality.
- **Minimize LED lights** - Those tiny green and red lights from electronics can be surprisingly disruptive. Cover them with electrical tape or remove electronics entirely.
- **Dimming capabilities** - Install dimmer switches or use lamps with multiple brightness settings to gradually decrease light in the evening.
- **Morning light strategy** - Consider a sunrise alarm clock that gradually brightens as morning approaches, helping your brain transition naturally from sleep to wake.

Managing Sound

Many of us with ADHD have auditory processing sensitivities that can make sleep challenging in anything less than perfect silence. Alternatively, some of us need consistent background noise to quiet our racing thoughts.

Here are some strategies to consider:

- **White noise machines** - These create a consistent sound backdrop that masks disruptive noises.
- **Earplugs** - Find comfortable ones designed for sleep if complete silence helps you rest.
- **Sleep headphones** - Soft headband-style headphones can be

comfortable for side sleepers who want to listen to meditation or white noise without disturbing others in the room.
- **Sound insulation** - Consider adding soft furnishings like rugs, curtains, and fabric wall hangings that absorb sound.

Touchy Feely

The physical comfort of your bed and bedroom can dramatically affect sleep quality. This goes beyond just a "comfortable mattress" to considering all the tactile elements of your sleep environment.

Essential strategies:

- **Bedding materials** - Experiment to find what works for you, from Egyptian cotton to satin.
- **Sleepwear** - If tags, seams, or certain fabrics bother you, honor that sensitivity. Consider whether you prefer sleeping with a pyjama, a gown, naked, or anything in between.
- **Weighted blankets** - Some ADHD folks find weighted blankets calming, while others feel trapped under them.
- **Temperature regulation** - Most sleep experts recommend a cool room (around 65-68°F/18-20°C) for optimal sleep, but warming it up in the morning helps getting out of bed.

3. KEEPING ELECTRONICS OUT (YES, SERIOUSLY)

> Pry my phone from my cold, dead hands, Estelle.

> I get it. Our phones have become like appendages of dopamine dispensers.

But I need to be crystal clear about this: electronics in the bedroom are sabotaging your sleep quality. This isn't up for discussion. The reasons are both obvious and subtle:

1. **Blue light disrupts melatonin production** - Blue light from screens effectively tells your brain it's still daytime.
2. **Content is stimulating** - Whether it's social media, news, emails, content engages your brain rather than allowing it to wind down.

3. **Notifications create alertness** - Even if your phone is silent, knowing it might buzz or light up keeps a part of your brain on alert.
4. **The "just one more" phenomenon** - ADHD brains are particularly susceptible to the "I'll just check one more thing" trap, which, thanks to time blindness, actually robs us of hours of sleep.

One of the most effective changes is to purchase an actual alarm clock. I leave my phone (on airplane mode) to charge in another room. I have seen a drastic improvement very quickly, in all my clients creating this simple change, not only in sleep but in their morning routine.

If you absolutely need to be on call for professional or personal reasons, consider other strategies:

- Use (or reconnect) your landline as an emergency line so you can still switch your mobile phone off.
- Leave your phone on but not right by your bed.
- Disable all non-urgent notifications like social media.
- Consider an app like AppBlock, Refocus, or Opal that can block certain apps at certain times. You can still receive phone calls or texts, but bye-bye doom scrolling.

4. THE 5-SECOND GAME CHANGER

And no, it's not "the 5-second rule." Besides buying an alarm clock, another quick win in the bedroom is to make your bed.

> Seriously, Estelle? Making my bed?

> What is this, military school?

> I know it sounds like a neurotypical mom's nagging advice, but hear me out.

You can make your bed in literally 5 seconds and reap all those benefits:

1. **Instant win** - Making your bed gives you an immediate, visible accomplishment first thing in the morning.

2. **Transition ritual** - A made bed signals to your brain that the sleep zone is now "closed for business" until bedtime.
3. **Reduces visual chaos** - Even if the rest of your room isn't perfectly organized, a made bed creates one large area of visual calm.
4. **More inviting later** - Especially when it's time to go to sleep.

The key to making this habit stick is simplicity. Forget elaborate arrangements with a trillion throw pillows, teddies (yes, grown-ups have 'decorative' teddies), and bedspreads. You only need one or two pillows per person and one duvet or sheet. Just pull, shake, throw. Job done!

FINAL THOUGHTS

Now, clothing clutter is a top bedroom issue, yet I've barely mentioned it so far. That's because the infamous floordrobe, where clean, dirty, and in-between clothes from mysterious archaeological layers across our bedroom floors, deserves special attention.

So let's dive into clothing organization, where we'll tackle everything from simplified wardrobes to laundry systems that actually work for ADHD brains.

KEY TAKEAWAYS

- **Sleep is your secret weapon**: One bad night can hijack your memory, attention, and emotional regulation. Treat sleep like a non-negotiable part of your ADHD management plan.
- **Start with zoning**: If your bedroom has to multitask, create clear boundaries between the sleep zone and other zones, using visual, physical, and sensory cues.
- **Sensory design changes everything**: Blackout curtains, cozy textures, calming smells, and the right sounds (or beautiful silence) can help regulate your nervous system and signal that it's safe to rest.
- **Hide what stresses**: Never work from your bed. Electronics are sleep thieves: Make a clean break by investing in a good old-fashioned alarm clock.
- **5-second win**: Making your bed is a micro-victory that sets the

tone. It signals closure on sleep, creates instant calm, and takes literal seconds.

CHAPTER ELEVEN
dressed without stress

KILL THE DECISION FATIGUE, AND FINALLY FIND YOUR PANTS

IF YOU'VE EVER FOUND yourself digging through a pile of clothes at 7:43 AM, desperately searching for something, anything, that's clean, unwrinkled, and socially acceptable for that 8:00 AM meeting (while your kids are asking where their clean socks are), you're not alone.

But here's the thing: once again, this isn't about shoulds or some arbitrary standard of tidiness. This is about how clothing chaos actively hijacks our executive function. Every morning that you're faced with that mountain of mixed-status clothing, your ADHD brain is forced to make dozens of unnecessary decisions before you've even had breakfast. And does it affect that 8 AM meeting we just mentioned? You bet.

Our brains have a limited capacity for decision-making each day, and wasting that precious resource on figuring out what to wear, or searching for that one specific shirt you know exists somewhere but where, means you have less mental bandwidth for the things that actually matter most to you.

So, when we talk about simplifying our clothing system, it's about deliberately reducing our mental load.

> Great! I'm ready to Marie Kondo my closet.

> Fab! But hold back fire.

> I've got a more ADHD friendly concept for you to avoid the clothes binge/purge cycle.

1. YOUR ULTIMATE CLOTHING HACK

And now the moment you've all been waiting for... the Capsule Wardrobe! Okay, maybe you're not as excited as I am about this. But as I mention it in pretty much all of my books, there was no way we would not take a deep dive into this when talking about organizing and cleaning!

A capsule wardrobe is the ultimate minimalist weapon. It's simply a curated collection of versatile pieces you love that fit well and can be mixed and matched effortlessly. It's not about being dull or lacking style, it's about making getting dressed require as little decision-making as possible.

ADHD-Friendly Capsule Wardrobe Guide

The ideal number is around 35-50 items per season (not counting basics like underwear, socks, and workout clothes). That might sound restrictive, but I promise it's liberating.

Here's a rough count:

- 5-7 tops for everyday wear
- 3-5 nicer tops for meetings or outings
- 4-7 bottoms (trousers, skirts, etc.)
- 1-5 dresses or jumpsuits (if you wear them)
- 4-7 layering pieces (cardigans, jackets, etc.)
- 2-5 pairs of shoes that go with everything
- A few select accessories that bring you joy

Remember: These numbers aren't sacred. The goal is a wardrobe where everything fits, everything works together, and getting dressed doesn't drain your executive function first thing in the morning.

If you're feeling overwhelmed and don't know where to start, here's a step-by-step guide to get you started. It doesn't have to be complicated.

7 Steps to Create Your Capsule Wardrobe:

1. **Think about your lifestyle** - Be honest about how you actually spend your time, not how you wish you spent it. If you work from home 90% of the time, you probably don't need 15 formal blazers. Just like we put intention in a room, have a little think about how you want your clothes to make you feel. Confident? Soothed?
2. **Start with what you have** - No need to buy a whole new wardrobe. You can 'shop your closet'. Select all your go-to and absolute favorites. Count the items and notice any gaps or abundance. Adapt accordingly, adding more or taking back from your donation pile.
3. **Pick a color palette** - Check for any color palette emerging from what you've selected. Capsule wardrobe purists recommend 2-3 base colors (like black, navy, gray, or beige) and 2-3 accent colors that make you happy and complement each other. This ensures almost everything can be mixed and matched. But don't overthink it at the beginning: it's likely to be the colors you already have or the ones when people say "you look great today." Once you've got rid of the clothes you don't wear (80%), you'll be able to see the 20% more clearly and streamline your palette.
4. **Focus on fit and fabric** - Fewer items mean each piece needs to pull its weight. Prioritize quality where you can, especially for items you wear frequently.
5. **Add personality** - Make sure your capsule reflects you. If you love vintage band t-shirts, incorporate them! If there is one piece that doesn't fit with anything else, but you love it? Keep it.
6. **Consider your sensory needs** - If certain fabrics, tags, or fits drive you crazy, eliminate them, no matter how "in fashion" or "essential" style guides claim they are.
7. **One Season at a time** - If you live somewhere with different seasons, start by creating your capsule wardrobe for the season you're in now. Put the rest in deep storage, and create a new capsule when the season changes. It avoids the mammoth tasks of planning four capsule wardrobes in one go. Then, once you've gone through the first year, use the seasonal rotation as an opportunity to keep clutter creep at bay.

Some items roll on over two or three seasons, a few lucky ones make it all year round, while the Christmas Sweater waits patiently for the winter capsule. I usually organically feel the need to change my capsule when the weather turns, but if you're worried you'll forget to take your sweaters and mittens out when it's freezing, you can put a reminder. Of course, this will look wildly different depending on where you live.

The Great Clothing Purge: Minimalism With Purpose

Now that you're armed with the knowledge to create a simplified wardrobe, let's eliminate those clothes that don't serve you anymore. Even if you're not ready for a full capsule wardrobe, I highly encourage you to downsize.

Most of us wear 20% of our clothes most of the time, yet our wardrobes remain stuffed with items we rarely touch. Of course, impulse buying is to blame, but also the sentimental attachment we might have to some items, the previously mentioned "just in case" lie, and let's not forget object permanence when we simply forget we already have it because we can't see it.

Let's be honest about what's really happening here. That Hawaiian shirt from your 2010 vacation that you've never worn since? It's not a cherished memory: it's an item taking up space and complicating your daily choices.

If you're going full-on capsule wardrobe, start by selecting your favorite clothes as mentioned above. Then come back here if you need a few more items or there are some pieces you're not sure about.

Then, for everyone, ask yourself our three key questions:

1. **Do I love it?** Does wearing this make you feel good? Comfortable? Confident? Or however else you want to feel.
2. **Do I need it?** Is it essential for your current life, not your fantasy life?
3. **Do I actually use it?** No matter how much you love it, have you worn it in the past year?

If the answer to all three is no, into the donation bag it goes. If you're wavering on something, remember, indecision is still a decision: it's a decision to keep letting that item take up physical and mental space.

> But Estelle, this designer jacket cost me a fortune!

> Yeah, but it's a sunk cost

That money is already spent, whether the item sits unworn in your closet or gets a second life with someone who'll actually use it. You might even be cutting losses by passing it on. Keeping expensive things you don't use is like paying rent for them to live in your home. They're taking up valuable mental and physical space that could be used for items you genuinely love and wear. And yes, you could try to sell it, but have an honest chat with yourself about whether it is worth your time.

2. CONQUERING THE LAUNDRY MONSTER

After you've reduced your amount of clothes, no matter which angle we take, eliminating the floordrobe (or chairdrobe) will also require a streamlined laundry process. Here are some basic principles to take you smoothly from piles scattered across your home to "clean in the closet".

Herding the Piles

The Half-Dirty Dilemma

The mysteries of the universe are, well, mysterious, and one of the bigger ones is: what to do with "half-dirty" clothes? You know what I'm talking about: those items that aren't quite dirty enough for the laundry but aren't quite clean enough to go back in the drawer.

I'll be very radical here and say there isn't such a thing. If it's clean enough for you to wear again, it's clean enough for your closet. If what I've just said grosses you out, then it belongs in the laundry basket. No half-measure is my best advice here.

Now, there is one modification that can be of interest. If you're happy to put it back in the wardrobe but worried you'll wear it too many times and not realize it's greying or starting to smell, put it back the wrong way around. Or, invest in a few hangers of a different color, especially for those "only wear once more then wash" items.

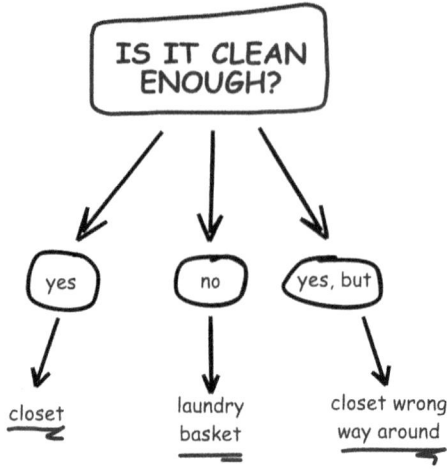

But what about loungewear? I'm not going to change them or fold them back every day?

A-ha! Excellent point.

For those kinds of exceptions, an over-door hook rack for your bedroom or bathroom door can be a great solution. Be very careful not to let it become a catch-all zone, though: decide what or how many items are allowed on the rack at the same time.

Strategic Placement

Remember my morning routine chaos, running from bedroom to bathroom and back for skincare and clothes? The same principle applies to laundry.

Where you place your laundry basket(s) will improve tremendously the chances of dirty clothes making it there. The most effective strategy to reduce friction is: Place baskets where clothes come off, not where they get washed. This might mean:

- A basket in each bedroom
- A basket in the bathroom
- A small hamper in the entryway for outdoor and/or exercising gear

Sort It Out

There's no right way to sort laundry. The best system is the one you'll actually maintain. But simplifying is the focus here again, and my general advice is to reduce the loads you need to do.

Here are some options to consider:

1. **One Load Per Person** - Each household member gets one load per week.

This works well for:

- Families where everyone does their own laundry or is more active in one part of the process, like folding or putting it back in the drawer.
    - Large houses where you don't want to run from one room to the other to pick and put things back.

2. **Sort by Color** - The traditional dark/light/colorful approach.

This works well for:

- People who wear a lot of new or vibrant clothes that might bleed
    - Those who want to keep their white proper white and their black proper black, and have different products and methods to achieve so.

3. **Sort by Fabric Type** - Group items by how they need to be spun/dried (delicates, heavy cottons, synthetics).

This works well for:

- People with varied wardrobes
    - Those concerned about clothing longevity
    - Anyone traumatized by a shrunken favorite woollen jumper
    - Anyone who wants to optimize for water/energy efficiency

4. **One-Size Fits All (or Just About)** - regular wash and occasional delicates.

This works well for:

- Busy people who need maximum simplicity
    - Those with mostly durable, modern clothing
    - Solo dwellers who want to keep to one load a week, most weeks

The Actual Washing: Schedule, Stack, Bundle

To make sure unfolded clean clothes don't accumulate as quickly as the dirty ones, deciding *when* you do laundry is more important than *how*. You need to find a good spot in your weekly reset.

Your main options are:

- **Batching** - Dedicate a weekend day (or an off day) to knock out all laundry at once. It works best if you don't have more than two loads.
- **Spread across a few days** - Either two off days or as part of your morning or evening routine. That's best if you have a lot of laundry or find large laundry sessions overwhelming.

Either way, use your machine's delay start feature to run laundry while you sleep or work. As we'll see, the real work starts after washing, so scheduling the end for when you're ready to tackle the next step makes a lot of sense.

Putting it Back

The No-Fold Revolution

I was once seduced by Marie Kondo's vertical folding technique. Seeing it all at once works great for the ADHD brain, and I liked the idea of optimizing space. But I soon realized that folding and putting clothes back in drawers was the hidden part of the laundry iceberg.

So I spent quite a lot of time testing how I could simplify the process as much as possible and reached another radical conclusion: you don't actually have to fold many things. Here is how:

- Thanks to the capsule wardrobe, you have created space, so you can hang almost everything: T-shirts, Jeans, sweaters, even tracksuits…

- Underwear and socks can be tossed in dedicated bins or drawer dividers. Pro tip: one type of socks per person (color, fabric, or other differentiation) = no more pairing socks. Or, just embrace the unmatched look.

The only ones left are items that go into deep storage or are used less frequently, like exercising outfits or loungewear. And even these, if they're not crinkling fabric, you can get away with bins and drawer dividers, or hang them if you still have space left.

Everything else? Find the ~~laziest~~ easiest, most effective method that works for you. And keep in mind task bundling too!

Utilize Drying

Dryers are convenient, but you could save time and drying loads with hanger drying: As most things end up hanging anyway, you can hang wet items and let them air dry. Then use the dryer for items you still fold or throw in dividers and heavier fabric (towels, sheets, etc).

This method eliminates an entire step in the laundry process and often reduces wrinkles, as well as your energy bill.

Beyond the clothes

So what about washing non-clothing fabric items? Towels, sheets, kitchen towels, etc.

With your dryer less busy with clothing items, you can adopt a same-day clean-and-return system:

1. Strip the bed in the morning
2. Wash and dry the sheets that same day
3. Put them right back on at night

Boom! Zero folding.

The same goes for towels and kitchen towels: Use, wash, and dry them when you don't need them, and start using them straight away.

Ironing

Just kidding. You really think the girl who's telling you not to fold has insights on ironing? I have nothing to say about ironing besides: don't do it!

No, okay, if you really press me (pun intended), you have three options:

1. **Don't do it** - If, like me, you hate it and don't require ironed shirts, don't own clothes that need ironing.
2. **Outsource** - If you hate it but need to wear crisp shirts, outsource the process to a specialized shop or someone coming to you a couple of hours a week.
3. **Bundle it** - If outsourcing is not an option or you don't hate it, it's like washing the dishes: either make it mindful or bundle it with something you love. Also, decide if you prefer a 3-minute job in the morning (if they are hang-dried, it can be that quick) or to batch your weekly load over the weekend while watching your favorite sitcom.

FINAL THOUGHTS

This isn't just about decluttering or finding your "style." It's about eliminating unnecessary friction in your life. It's about removing those tiny-but-draining decisions, those daily stumbles over piles of laundry, that silent shame whispering from your floordrobe. You don't have to fold if folding breaks your brain. You don't have to keep that blazer just because it was expensive. And you certainly don't have to iron. (I mean… really.)

What you *do* have to do is this: build a system that works for *you*. Whether you're creating your first capsule wardrobe or just moving your laundry basket two feet closer to where your clothes come off, you're making it a whole lot easier on your executive function and shifting toward a life that supports your brain.

Now that we've sorted your threads, it's time to tackle another beast: your workspace. Yes, both the physical *and* the digital kind. Because those piles of paper, notification pings, and 87 open browser tabs are draining your focus just as much as your sock mountain.

KEY TAKEAWAYS

- **Clothing clutter hijacks your executive function** - Every "what do I wear?" moment drains your mental energy, simplifying your wardrobe frees up precious bandwidth for the stuff that actually matters.

- **A capsule wardrobe is your new best friend** - With 35–50 mix-and-match pieces per season, getting dressed becomes effortless and decision-fatigue-free. Pick clothes that fit *how* you actually live and how you want to *feel*. Starting with what you already have: pick what you love and need and let go of "just in case" clothes.
- **Laundry systems must reduce friction** - The "half-dirty" category is a myth. Clothes are either clean enough to wear again or not. Place baskets where clothes come off, sort in a way that works for your brain, and schedule laundry in ways that align with your natural energy.
- **No folding, no ironing** - Seriously. Hang most clothes, toss undies in bins, and ditch the perfectionism. You are not required to iron. Ever. But if you must: outsource it, keep it minimal and strategic, or…
- **Bundle it** - Pair laundry folding (or hanging) with something fun: podcasts, audiobooks, music, your comfort show.

CHAPTER TWELVE
a working workspace
HOW TO CREATE A PRODUCTIVE ENVIRONMENT (DIGITALLY AND IN REAL LIFE)

BY NOW, you're no stranger to environment design. We've explored how our spaces affect our ADHD brains and the importance of creating zones that serve specific purposes. Your workspace, whether it's a dedicated home office, a corner of your dining table, or a cubicle in a corporate building, deserves the same intentional approach.

1. ENVIRONMENT DESIGN FOR MAXIMUM FOCUS

Just like your other zones, a workspace has a primary purpose, and that's likely to be supporting productivity. But here's where it gets personal: what "productive" looks like for your specific ADHD brain might be quite different from what it looks like for another ADHD brain.

Set Up

For many of us with ADHD, a minimalist workspace is the key to focus. While I love affirmations and motivational quotes in other contexts, my workspace remains deliberately free of them.

So, what essentials do you need? Here are a few ideas to choose from:

- Computer
- Noise canceling-headphones

- Post-it notes, notebook, or notepad (to jot down anything without the distraction of an app)
- A few good pens
- Sensory relief: hand cream, fidgets, scented candle, daylight bulb, or lamp
- Plant (to boost the mood)
- Clock (to help with time-blindness)
- Water bottle (to stay hydrated during hyperfocus deep work sessions)
- Flask of tea or coffee (so you don't get distracted when going to the kitchen)

The point is to think critically about what *you* need to achieve maximum productivity. Of course, it might need a bit of trial and error, and this is a setup you can work with over time.

Ergonomics

Let's talk about an overlooked game-changer: ergonomics. When your body is comfortable, your mind can focus instead of constantly registering discomfort.

Here are some ergonomic options worth considering:

- **Hydraulic or standing desk** - The ability to change positions throughout the day keeps restless bodies and minds happy
- **An under-desk bike, stepper, or treadmill** - For more active engagement
- **Exercise ball chairs** - To wiggle while thinking
- **Inflatable seat cushions** - These provide the benefits of an exercise ball for standard chairs
- **Ergonomic kneeling chairs** - Promote better posture and core engagement
- **Wrist pads** - Prevent strain during extended typing sessions
- **Footrests** - Particularly rocking footrests provide sensory input while seated
- **Monitor risers** - Position screens at eye level to prevent neck strain
- **Fidgets** - The additional tactile input can help focus the mind when reading, listening, or in a meeting

Remember, the best ergonomic setup is the one that works for your unique body and sensory needs. If you thrive with movement, prioritize solutions that allow for it. If stability helps you focus, invest in supportive, comfortable seating.

Sensory Design

Just like we've seen in the bedroom, the sensory environment of your workspace can make a huge difference.

Lighting

Lighting isn't just about seeing clearly; it profoundly affects mood, focus, and energy levels. Consider these lighting elements:

- **Natural light** - Position near windows when possible, but with the ability to filter bright direct sun
- **A sunlight lamp** - The perfect tool that mimics natural light to combat seasonal depression.
- **Light temperature** - Cooler, blue-toned light tends to promote alertness, while warmer light can be calming
- **Anti-glare screens** - Reduce eye strain and headaches from screen use
- **Task lighting** - Directional lighting that illuminates your work area without creating ambient brightness
- **Dimmable options** - Allow adjustment based on time of day and task type

Sound Environment

Noise-canceling headphones are non-negotiable in my workspace toolkit. They provide an invaluable layer of control over my auditory environment.

Consider what sound environment best supports your focus:

- **Complete silence** - Some ADHD brains focus best with minimal auditory input
- **White noise** - Creates a consistent sound floor that masks distracting noises
- **Lyric-free music** - Provides stimulation without the distraction of words

- **Nature sounds** - Can have a calming effect on the nervous system
- **Binaural beats** - A 2022 pilot trial evaluating the effect of binaural beats on study performance, mind-wandering, and core symptoms of adult ADHD patients concluded that "Binaural Beats seem to improve subjective studying performance and ADHD symptoms severity"

You can find most of those on playlist streaming, or for tailored binaural beats sessions, you can subscribe to an App like Endell or brain.fm

Advocate Like Pro

Many of these ergonomic and sensory tools can be considered reasonable workplace adjustments for ADHD.

Depending on your employer, country, and local laws, you may be entitled to support for these accommodations. Some workplaces can offer consultations with ergonomic specialists, and even if you're self-employed, you might be entitled to a grant for some of those adjustments. These aren't luxury items; they're tools that help create an equitable working environment for neurodivergent brains to do their best work.

Besides those adjustments, if you share your workspace with others, whether at home or in an office, you'll need to navigate competing needs and preferences. Regardless of neurodivergence, everybody has ways of working best, so always address those as conversations where everybody can share their needs:

- Be explicit: never assume that others understand what you need or feel
- Share from your perspective. For instance, "I work better with fewer visual distractions" rather than "Your stuff is everywhere."
- Propose specific, solution-oriented ideas and use " how can we" to compromise creatively.

Keeping these conversations on mutual benefit rather than criticism can make them much more productive.

2. PAPER MANAGEMENT: THE PHYSICAL INBOX

No discussion of workspace design would be complete without addressing the paper monster: bills, mail, notes, and documents seem to multiply and migrate across every surface when we're not looking.

The Simplest Filing System Ever

If you've been intimidated by complex filing systems with color-coding and dozens of categories, I have liberating news: you don't need all that. Here's the simplest filing system that actually works:

1. **Forever Documents** - One folder for items you'll need permanently (birth certificates, property deeds, marriage licenses, will, etc.)
2. **Current Year** - One folder per year for everything else that needs keeping "just in case"

Keep these yearly folders for 12 years, or whichever is the longest statutory time out of all your papers (check whatever is appropriate in your location to be on the legal safe side), then discard them.

This system eliminates the paralyzing "Where should I file this?" question that often leads to papers piling up unprocessed. In most cases, you will never need them. And if you do, you'll spend a few minutes in that year folder.

The One-Touch Rule

The idea is to handle each piece of paper exactly once. When a document comes into your possession, immediately decide its fate:

1. **Act on it now** - Pay the bill, fill out the form, sign the document
2. **File it** - Put it in your simplified filing system immediately
3. **Discard it** - Be ruthless: most paper can be recycled or shredded

This approach eliminates the infamous "I'll deal with this later" pile that somehow never gets dealt with.

If the one-touch rule feels impossible because mail arrives at inconvenient times, create a designated inbox for paper and schedule a specific weekly time to process it all. This could be part of your work schedule or your weekly home organization reset.

The ultimate paper solution? Eliminate it entirely and opt for electronic statements and bills. Having said that, digital clutter is absolutely real, and we'll address it right now. But digital documents are generally easier to search, don't take up physical space, and can't get coffee spilled on them.

3. DIGITAL CLUTTER: TAMING THE INVISIBLE MONSTER

While physical clutter might be more immediately visible, digital clutter has become an even more insidious productivity killer for many of us. Our devices offer endless opportunities for distraction, overwhelm, and procrastination, all wrapped in convenient, pocket-sized packages that follow us everywhere.

Let's tackle the three biggest culprits of digital clutter: emails, phone apps, and computer desktops.

Four Steps to Email Management

Emails are essentially the digital equivalent of paper piles: they accumulate rapidly, create visual overwhelm, and often contain a mix of important information, tasks to complete, and complete junk.

Most productivity experts agree on one fundamental email practice: stop checking email constantly throughout the day. Having your email open continuously is disastrous for anyone's focus, let alone ADHD brains.

It's a particularly seductive trap for us, because of the element of surprise, the "what will I find" uncertainty that delivers a little dopamine hit each time. But this habit destroys our ability to focus on meaningful work as we struggle with task-switching.

Instead, try batch processing:

Step 1: Schedule it

- Plan 1-3 email sessions per day when you check and process.
- Schedule these check-ins based on your work rhythm. But

generally speaking, avoid checking first thing in the morning. Pick a time after a deep work session to be more productive.

Step 2: Sort it

Use the 3 Ds strategy for emails that take under 3 minutes:

- Delete it: Get rid of anything unnecessary
- Deal with it: Respond immediately if it's quick
- Delegate it: Forward to someone else if appropriate

For emails requiring more than 3 minutes:

- Schedule a specific time to address it
- Move it to a folder so it's not clogging your inbox (but only if it is scheduled somewhere, or out of sight... More on folders in step 3)

This is essentially the one-touch rule we discussed for physical paper, applied to digital communications. The goal is to prevent repeatedly seeing the same emails without taking action, which creates inbox overflow, mental load, and anxiety.

Step 3: File it

Just like with paper, simplicity is key:

1. Create two to three basic folders for the current year. You could pick from those:
    - Current affairs (for emails you will need soon: proof of purchase, bookings, waiting to hear back from
    - someone, scheduled to be processed, etc.
    - Newsletters you want to read later
    - Receipts
    - Professional
    - Personal
    - Everything else
2. At the end of the year, apply the same yearly filing system that you do for paper
    - Create a forever folder
    - Create an archive year folder
    - Move emails you need to keep into the correct folder and delete the others

- Keep your yearly folder for your required retention period (usually 10-12 years)

Step 4: Unsubscribe

45% of most inboxes consist of marketing emails and newsletters. Many of which never get opened?

Be ruthless with the unsubscribe button. Keep only newsletters and updates that genuinely bring you value or joy. For everything else, unsubscribe immediately when they appear in your inbox (and yes, I'm including myself: unsubscribe from my emails if they're not valuable).

If your inbox is completely out of control, consider using a tool like Unroll.me, Clean Email, or againstdata.com that can help you bulk unsubscribe and delete.

Phone Organization: Your Pocket Distraction Machine

Our phones have evolved from simple communication tools to dopamine dispensers that we carry everywhere. Creating some intentional friction between you and distracting apps can dramatically improve both focus and mental health.

Notification Detox

Start with the simplest change: turn off notifications for anything that isn't truly urgent. Ask yourself: "Does this app deserve the right to interrupt my thoughts at any moment?"

For most apps, such as social media, games, news, and group chats, the answer is a resounding no. Keep notifications only for direct communications from actual humans (texts, calls) and reminders you have set up.

Remove Temptation

Here are three options to create distance between you and your phone, or you and certain apps.

Option 1: Total Detox

For a more radical reset, try a complete digital detox:

1. Remove everything except essential communication tools (phone, messages).
2. After four weeks, selectively reinstall only the apps you genuinely missed and that add value to your life.

Option 2: Home Screen Makeover

Your home screen should support your goals, not undermine them. Consider:

- Removing or hiding distracting apps (on iPhone, you can hide apps without deleting them, making them accessible through search but not visible)
- Putting helpful, goal-supporting apps (like productivity tools, exercise trackers, meditation apps) front and center
- Burying distracting apps several screens deep or in folders

Option 2: App Blockers and Focus Tools

Tools like Freedom, Opal, or AppBlock can create scheduled periods of focus by temporarily blocking distracting apps and websites.

These create an external accountability and can be a great solution if you can't switch your phone in case of an emergency, but want to mentally switch off from digital life.

Computer Organization: Digital Desktop Design

The principles we've applied to physical spaces and phones work equally well for your computer organization.

A cluttered desktop creates the same visual overwhelm as a cluttered physical desk. The goal is to have very few icons visible on your desktop. Only the tools you use daily should earn that placement.

Folders

Create a system of main folders that mirrors your life:

- Personal folder
- Work folder
- Hobbies folder

Within these, you can create yearly subfolders similar to your paper and email systems.

Applications

Just like with your phone, keep only your most productive and necessary applications visible and easily accessible:

- Pin only essential apps to your taskbar or dock
- Hide rarely used or distracting applications in folders

Digital Work Environment

Beyond organization, consider how your digital work environment affects your focus:

- Use focus modes or full-screen applications to minimize distractions
- Consider website blockers during work sessions

Digital Maintenance: Preventing Re-Clutter

Just like physical spaces, digital environments need regular maintenance to prevent clutter from accumulating again. Consider adding these to your regular resets:

- Weekly email cleanup (15 minutes)
- Monthly phone app review (delete unused apps)
- Quarterly computer file organization
- Annual digital decluttering day, where you delete or archive what's in that yearly folder (photos, downloads, old documents)

Digital clutter might be invisible, but its impact is very, very real. Whether it's the endless notifications, an overflowing inbox, or a desktop so cluttered you can't see your wallpaper anymore, every bit adds up and chips away at your focus, calm, and executive function. But just like with physical spaces, you don't need perfection; you need clarity, simplicity, and habits that support the way your brain actually works.

FINAL THOUGHTS

Your workspace is not just where tasks happen, whether it's a sunlit home office, a corner of the dining table, or the only uncluttered two square feet left on your kitchen counter. It's where your ideas come to life, where your energy is either drained or refilled, and where your ADHD brain either flounders… or flies.

In this chapter, we've created a physical and digital space that supports the way your brain works. We've looked at sensory design, ergonomics, productivity tools, and communication. We've faced down the paper monster. And we've wrestled with digital chaos, those sneaky little energy vampires that pretend to be productive while quietly devouring your focus.

And now? You've got options. You've got strategies. You've got small tweaks that add up to significant change. It's about creating an environment that makes your life easier, your work more focused, and your brain a little calmer.

KEY TAKEAWAYS

- **Your workspace deserves intention**: Just like every other zone in your home, your workspace (no matter how tiny or shared) can be designed to support how your ADHD brain actually works, not how it "should."
- **Function over fluff**: Keep only what you truly use and need on your desk. Standing desks, wobbly stools, rocking footrests… these aren't indulgences, they're legit tools for focus and comfort, especially for ADHD bodies that love to move.
- **Sensory design makes or breaks your focus**: Whether it's natural light, white noise, or a particular scent, tailoring your workspace to your sensory needs isn't a luxury. If you're sharing your workspace (at home or at the office), open conversations about needs and adjustments can make everyone more productive.
- **Keep paper ridiculously simple**: One folder for forever documents. One folder per year for the rest. Whether it's paper mail or digital files, aim to act on it, file it, or delete it the first time you open it. "Later" is where clutter goes to die.
- **Digital clutter is real**: Overflowing inboxes, 42 browser tabs, and app chaos are not invisible. They drain your focus just like

piles on your desk. Simplify your screens like you simplify your drawers.
- **Your phone is not your boss**: Turn off non-essential notifications. Move distracting apps off your home screen. Use blockers if you need them.

week 4 tasks: creating adhd-friendly spaces

DAY 1

- Do your daily reset
- Do your relevant weekly reset (e.g., laundry day)
- Find FIFTEEN things to declutter
- Environment Modifications: Focus on the Top Priority Zone you've decluttered. What small changes could you make to support your brain better? Consider lighting, sound, visual clutter, or comfort. Choose just ONE modification you could implement today. Jot down the others for later
- Plan how you will treat yourself at the end of the 28 days

DAY 2

- Do your daily reset
- Do your relevant weekly reset
- Find SIXTEEN things to declutter
- Storage Refinement: Review your storage tiers (1-4) in your current Top Priority Zone. Is anything in the wrong tier? Should daily items be more visible? Should occasional items be tucked away? Make one small adjustment to improve your system
- Improve your daily reset: How can you make it easier? More efficient? More fun?

DAY 3

- Do your daily reset
- Do your relevant weekly reset
- Find SEVENTEEN things to declutter
- Sensory Improvement: What sensory element could you adjust in your space to make it more comfortable? This might be adding a cushion, changing a light bulb, introducing a pleasant scent, or reducing noise. Choose something simple that you can implement today

- Consider moving to another priority zone to declutter. Where would have the most impact next?

DAY 4

- Do your daily reset
- Do your relevant weekly reset
- Find EIGHTEEN things to declutter
- Digital Clutter: Take one step to tackle some digital clutter. Delete unused apps, unsubscribe from newsletters you never read, or clear your desktop
- Look at your Top Priority Zone(s): Once they're decluttered, consider environment or sensory adjustments to get closer to your desired feeling (e.g., blackout curtains, moisturizer by the bedside lamp, clock on your desk, etc.). Do it now or schedule it

DAY 5

- Do your daily reset
- Do your relevant weekly reset
- Find NINETEEN things to declutter
- Clothing System: Wherever you keep your clothes, consider implementing (or refining) your capsule wardrobe. Or at least downsize your closet. Reflect on your laundry system? Could you simplify your sorting or minimize folding?
- Consider moving to another zone to declutter. Where would have the most impact next?

DAY 6

- Do your daily reset
- Do your relevant weekly reset
- Find TWENTY things to declutter
- Habit Helper: What small addition or change could make your daily routine easier? Choose one simple modification that reduces friction in your daily life
- Improve your weekly reset: How can you make it easier? More efficient? More fun?

DAY 7

- Do your daily reset
- Do your relevant weekly reset
- Find TWENTY-ONE things to declutter
- Take your stuff to the charity shop or tip, and empty your bins
- Plan for maintenance: What are your resets now? Do you still need to declutter? If yes, pick one of the challenges or set a certain number per day or week. If not, plan how you're going to incorporate decluttering in your resets
- Celebration Time! Reflect on how much you've accomplished in these 28 days! What systems are working well? What habits have you built? What impact has this had on your daily life and ADHD symptoms?

Congratulations on completing the 28-day framework! Remember, your home should work for your unique ADHD brain, not against it. Keep experimenting, stay curious, and celebrate every win, no h small!

in conclusion

You're now standing on the edge of something new, surrounded by the scattered remains of old systems, old shame, and old stories you no longer need to carry.

Over the past chapters, we've wandered together through the realities of ADHD and mess: not just the physical clutter, but the emotional weight, the executive dysfunction, and the silent self-criticism that tends to hum in the background. And step by step, room by room, layer by layer, you started to lift it.

You've learned that your brain isn't the problem. The systems you were taught? The unrealistic expectations? The one-size-fits-no-one checklists? Those were the problems.

Maybe you started this book feeling overwhelmed. Maybe you were sitting in a kitchen that made you want to cry or a bedroom you hadn't truly rested in for years. Maybe, if we're being really honest, you didn't believe a book could change anything.

You've faced the overwhelm that so often feels like a tidal wave and said, "Not today." You've peeled back the labels (lazy, chaotic, careless) and replaced them with clarity. And you did it not by trying to become someone else, but by working with your ADHD brain, not against it.

You saw how creating zones helps your brain know what happens where. You've learned to ditch perfectionism in favour of function. You've shifted from cleaning frenzies to reset rituals, and from guilt to gentle momentum. You've turned "I should" into "how can I?" You built a lived-in, ADHD-friendly space that supports your body, focus, rest, and joy.

You've navigated the rooms that often trip us up the most: the kitchen that decides whether we eat or spiral; the bathroom, where our day begins and ends; the bedroom, which should offer rest, not resentment. You decluttered your closet not just to see the floor again, but to eliminate decision fatigue. You faced down laundry systems, reset rituals, and let go of the idea that "clean" has to mean "perfect."

You also looked beyond the visible mess, into the invisible monsters that live in your phone, your inbox, your digital workspace, the buzzing notifications that promise dopamine but deliver distraction. ADHD clutter doesn't just live on our coffee tables; it lives in our browsers and brains.

You took back your focus, not through willpower, but through strategy. You learned how to reduce friction, make decisions once, and create boundaries, with stuff, with screens, and sometimes, with people.

And let's not forget: you learned how to clean with others, not despite them. You rethought how to involve children without bribery or power struggles. You learned to communicate your needs clearly and share the mental load in ways that honour everyone's differences, including your own.

So, what now?

That's your call. This work isn't about arriving at a final destination where everything stays clean and calm forever. That doesn't exist, not for anyone, ADHD or not. But now you know how to restart without spiralling. You've got scaffolding. You've got compassion. You've got a system that can bend without breaking.

Maybe you keep building on the systems you've created. Maybe you rest for a while. Maybe you revisit these pages when the clutter creeps back in. You can always come back. You're always allowed to begin again. You might reach out for extra support, and if that's you, you know where to find me, whether it's through the Empowering ADHD Club, a future book, or my emails cheering you on.

Your space is not a test. Your worth is not in your laundry basket. You're not behind. You're becoming.

found your floor? pay it forward!

Did you manage to find your floor again? Perhaps even reclaim a sense of control you thought was lost forever?

Leaving a review is like handing a comforting map to the next ADHD adventurer feeling overwhelmed in their own clutter jungle. Your experience can help someone else realize that clarity and peace are possible.

Not sure what to say? You could share:

- A specific organizing success that surprised or delighted you
- Your favorite strategy or exercise from the book
- How is the 28-day format making the path to an organized space feel doable?

Ready to help someone else find their way from chaos to calm?

Here's how easy it is to leave your review:

1. Click this link or scan the QR code: mybook.to/ADHDorganization
2. Scroll down to the review section.
3. Click on "Write a Customer Review," just beneath the ratings.

That's it! It takes less time than losing (and then finding) your favorite sock, and your words might be exactly what someone needs to begin their own journey toward a supportive space.

IT'S NOT TOO LATE

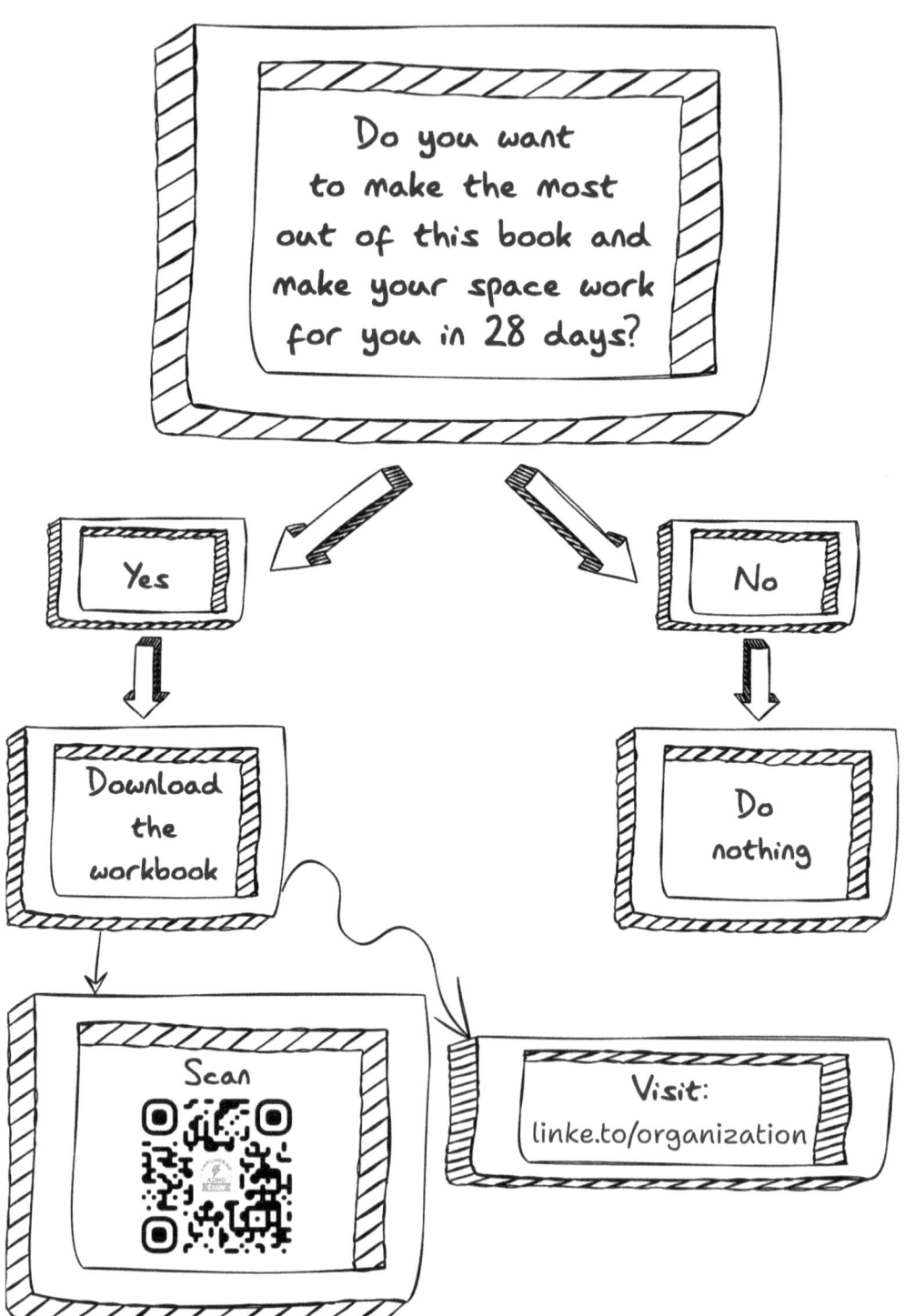

also by estelle rose

Hey there! If Adult ADHD Executive Function 7-Week Power-Up gave you a spark of hope and momentum, I've got more where that came from. Let me introduce you to a few of my other books—think of them as the squad that's got your back, ready to help you tackle life with ADHD in the most practical, empowering, and sometimes laugh-out-loud way.

ADULT ADHD EXECUTIVE FUNCTION 7-WEEK POWER-UP: YOUR TOOLKIT TO ENHANCE FOCUS, MANAGE TIME, AND BOOST PRODUCTIVITY

Feeling stuck in a cycle of procrastination and stress? This step-by-step program helps you identify your biggest executive function roadblocks and gives you tailored tools to tackle them. With quick wins, bite-sized strategies, and assessments to keep you on course, you'll learn how to harness hyperfocus, manage impulsivity, and build systems that stick—without the pressure of rigid timelines. It's like having a coach in your corner, cheering you on while you make progress at your own pace.

The Empowering ADHD Workbook for Women: Embrace Your Brilliance Without the Burnout

This one's a game-changer if you're ready to dig deep and tackle the stuff that really holds us back—think self-esteem, confidence, and those never-ending racing thoughts. It's packed with hands-on tools, downloadable trackers, and beautifully illustrated pages designed for our neurospicy brains (same illustrator as Empowered Women With ADHD—more on that in a sec). Plus, we're talking career and finance advice, emotional regulation, and clutter-busting tips you can actually stick to. If the current book is about getting your executive functions humming, this one's about reconnecting with you—your confidence, your calm, and your power.

Empowered Women With ADHD: Unlock Your Full Potential with Proven Tools and Strategies

This one's like your candid, no-judgment BFF who gets what it's like to live on the ADHD rollercoaster. We're slowing down the racing thoughts, setting boundaries (without the guilt), and creating space to thrive at work and in relationships. The illustrations are back, too—just as fun and supportive as before. Whether you're feeling stuck in hyperfocus or overwhelmed by hyper-fatigue, this book will meet you where you are and help you make ADHD work for you instead of against you.

Brain-Boosting Foods for Women with ADHD: Nourish Your Focus, Mood, and Energy

Let's talk about food (and yes, snacks). If brain fog and low energy are slowing you down, this book has your back with a nutrition-focused guide to ADHD-friendly eating. You'll find affordable, accessible ingredients, quick recipes (we're talking under 15 minutes), and week-by-week meal plans that make eating for focus and clarity a breeze. Say goodbye to that "traffic jam" feeling in your brain and hello to more energy, better mood, and recipes you'll actually want to make.

I wrote these books because I've been in the trenches, too—trying to juggle all the things while feeling like I'm constantly losing my grip. If you're ready for practical tools, a little bit of laughter, and a whole lot of *you've got this* energy, these books are here to help.

Let's keep this momentum going—your brilliance is just getting started.

about the author

Estelle Rose is a certified coach (DBT + EFT practitioner) and the author of bestselling guides like *The Empowering ADHD Workbook for Women*.

Diagnosed late after years of high-functioning overwhelm, she gets what it's like to look like you've got it all together while secretly struggling to keep up.

With a mix of empathy, humor, neuroscience, coaching strategies, and lived experience, Estelle offers clear, compassionate support to make sense of ADHD and become more productive with less pressure.

Explore her latest book or join her support community, *The Empowering ADHD Club*.

estelle-rose.com

bibliography

Aarts, H., & Custers, R. (2012). Unconscious Goal Pursuit: Nonconscious Goal Regulation and Motivation. https://doi.org/10.1093/OXFORDHB/9780195399820.013.0014.

Abdaal, A. (2025). *Feel-Good Productivity: How to Do More of What Matters to You*. Penguin Group.

Clear, J. (2018). *Atomic Habits: An easy & proven way to build good habits & break bad ones*. Random House Business.

Custers, R., Vermeent, S., & Aarts, H. (2019). Does Goal Pursuit Require Conscious Awareness?. *The Oxford Handbook of Human Motivation*. https://doi.org/10.1093/oxfordhb/9780190666453.013.15.

Durand, G., Arbone, I., & Wharton, M. (2020). Reduced organizational skills in adults with ADHD are due to deficits in persistence, not in strategies. *PeerJ*, 8. https://doi.org/10.7717/peerj.9844.

Fargason, R., Fobian, A., Hablitz, L., Paul, J., White, B., Cropsey, K., & Gamble, K. (2017). Correcting delayed circadian phase with bright light therapy predicts improvement in ADHD symptoms: A pilot study. *Journal of psychiatric research*, 91, 105-110. https://doi.org/10.1016/j.jpsychires.2017.03.004.

Holst, Y., & Thorell, L. (2020). Functional impairments among adults with ADHD: A comparison with adults with other psychiatric disorders and links to executive deficits. *Applied Neuropsychology: Adult*, 27, 243 - 255. https://doi.org/10.1080/23279095.2018.1532429.

Kooij, J., Bijlenga, D., Brown, G., Someren, E., , N., Streiner, D., & , M. (2014). High Prevalence of Self-Reported Photophobia in Adult ADHD. Frontiers in Neurology, 5. https://doi.org/10.3389/fneur.2014.00256.

Lasky, A., Weisner, T., Jensen, P., Hinshaw, S., Hechtman, L., Arnold, L., Murray, D., & Swanson, J. (2016). ADHD in context: Young adults' reports of the impact of occupational environment on the manifestation of ADHD.. *Social science & medicine*, 161, 160-8 . https://doi.org/10.1016/j.socscimed.2016.06.003.

Malandrone, F., Spadotto, M., Boero, M., Bracco, I. F., & Oliva, F. (2022). A pilot add-on Randomized-Controlled Trial evaluating the effect of binaural beats on study performance, mind-wandering, and core symptoms of adult ADHD patients. *European Psychiatry*, 65(S1), S274–S274. doi:10.1192/j.eurpsy.2022.701

Robbins, M. (2017). *The 5 Second Rule: Transform Your Life, Work, and Confidence with Everyday Courage*. Savio Republic.

Rosario-Hernández, E., & Rovira-Millán, L. (2020). ADHD and its Effects on Job Performance: A Moderated Mediation Model. *Spring*. https://doi.org/10.37226/rcp.2020/01.

Stein, M. A., & Weiss, M. D. (2023). Editorial: Longitudinal Associations Between Sleep and ADHD Symptoms: ADHD Is a 24-Hour Disorder. *Journal of the American Academy of Child and Adolescent Psychiatry*, 62(2), 133–134. https://doi.org/10.1016/j.jaac.2022.11.003

White, E., DeBoer, M., & Scharf, R. (2019). Associations Between Household Chores and Childhood Self-Competency. *Journal of Developmental & Behavioral Pediatrics*, 40, 176–182. https://doi.org/10.1097/DBP.0000000000000637.

Williamson, A. M., & Feyer, A. M. (2000). Moderate sleep deprivation produces impairments in cognitive and motor performance equivalent to legally prescribed levels of alcohol intoxication. *Occupational and environmental medicine, 57*(10), 649–655. https://doi.org/10.1136/oem.57.10.649

www.ingramcontent.com/pod-product-compliance
Lightning Source LLC
Chambersburg PA
CBHW070804040426
42333CB00061B/2192